123 Champagne Recipes

(123 Champagne Recipes - Volume 1)

Wendy Beran

Content

123 Awesome Champagne Recipes

***

1. A Refined «thirst Satisfying» Summer Party Drink.

Serving: Serves 6-8 | Prep: | Cook: | Ready in:

Ingredients

- • 1 pint fresh wiled or small strawberries
- • 2 tablespoons White Rum or any good alcohol
- • 1/3 cup superfine sugar
- • 1 bottle champagne

Direction

- Fill a large bowl with ice cubes. Place strawberries in a smaller bowl, sprinkle with Rum and sugar and put on top of the ice for about 30 to 45 minutes before serving.
- To serve; put a few strawberries in the bottom of wide champagne glasses and at the table fill with champagne.

2. Ahi Tuna With Angel Hair Pasta

Serving: Serves 4 | Prep: | Cook: | Ready in:

Ingredients

- Ingredients for the Pasta
- 1 pound angel hair pasta
- 1 small shallot, diced
- 1 zucchini, chopped
- 1/2 cup red bell pepper, thinly sliced
- 1/2 cup mini-roma tomatoes, cut in half (or cherry tomatoes)
- 3 tablespoons champagne vinegar
- 1/4 cup olive oil, divided
- 1/4 cup reserved pasta water
- Fresh cilantro
- Ingredients for Tuna
- 1 tablespoon spanish paprika
- 2 teaspoons ground coriander
- 1 teaspoon dried oregano
- 1 teaspoon chili powder
- 1 1/2 teaspoons ground mustard
- Olive oil for searing
- 4 (4 oz) fillets of ahi tuna

Direction

- Cook the pasta by following the package less 2 minutes and set aside in a bowl. You can add a little water or olive oil while it sits. Reserve 1 cup of pasta water.
- Take a large sauté pan over medium heat and add in 1 tablespoon olive oil. Add in shallot and cook for 2 minutes. Next add in zucchini and bell pepper. Let sauté for 4 minutes. Turn heat off and add in tomatoes and champagne vinegar. Let sit until tuna is ready.
- In a small bowl combine paprika, coriander, oregano, chili powder and ground mustard. Move to a plate and coat each tuna on both sides. Set aside.
- Heat your indoor grill pan over medium-high heat. Once hot add in olive oil to coat the bottom of the pan. Add tuna and sear for 2-3 minutes (depending on the thickness). Flip over and turn off heat and let the fish heat through.
- Take the pan with the vegetables and turn to medium heat. Once hot add in pasta, 2 tablespoons olive oil and using thongs to combine ingredients. Add in cilantro and if you need more liquid add some pasta water 1 tablespoon at a time. Taste for any additional seasonings.
- On a board, slice tuna.

- To serve add pasta to the bottom of the plate and divide the tuna pieces to 4 plates.

3. Artichoke And Champagne Risotto Risotto Con I Carciofi Allo Champagne

Serving: Serves 4-6 | Prep: | Cook: | Ready in:

Ingredients

- 2 cups Carnaroli fine rice (not parboiled)
- 4 to 5 cups vegetable broth
- 1/2 cup Champagne (brut)
- 2 tablespoons Extra Virgin Olive Oil
- 6 medium artichokes
- 1 lemon in juice
- 1 yellow onion very finely chopped
- 2 garlic cloves, finely chopped, green inner part removed
- 1 tablespoon fresh parsley finely chopped
- 6 tablespoons Parmesan cheese grated
- Black pepper
- Salt

Direction

- Fill a bowl with cold water and add the juice of one lemon.
- To clean and trim the artichokes (you can wear rubber gloves as artichokes stain your hands): Trim and pair the artichokes until you are left with only the very tender part (the heart and the initial light green part of the leaves. Cut in thin wedges and put in the bowl with lemon juice so they don't get dark.
- Peel and chop very finely the onion. Do the same with the garlic cloves, removing the inner fibrous part) and keep them in separate bowls. Chop the parsley and set aside.
- Put the vegetable broth in a pan and keep it over low heat so it is always hot. You might not need all of it, depends on the quality of the rice you use.

- In a pan with a tight fitting lid, melt half the butter over medium heat, add the onion and allow to cook for 5 minutes until translucent. Add the artichokes and the garlic, season with salt and let simmer, covering the pan with the lid for 7 to 8 minutes. Add the champagne, stir and let the alcohol evaporate completely.
- In a large frying pan, over medium-high heat, add the olive oil and fry the rice until well coated in oil and slightly translucent.
- Add the rice to the artichokes and stir together. Season with salt and pepper, add enough broth to just cover the rice and artichokes, lower the heat to medium-low and allow to cook uncovered until it's almost dry. Add another ladle of broth and stir. Allow to simmer gently until it's almost dry again. Keep repeating the process, adding less and less stock every time you add it to the risotto.
- After 15 minutes, remove from the heat, add a tiny quantity of broth, the parsley, the Parmesan, the remaining butter, stir vigorously with a wooden spoon, cover and let rest for 2 or 3 minutes before serving.
- You can have the artichokes prepared ahead and in water and lemon juice 2 days in the fridge and just make the risotto when you intend to serve it.
- NOTE FOR COOKING AHEAD: If you want to do ahead the risotto proceed until you have a pre-cooked rice, that is, until you add the first ladle of broth. Bring to a boil, cover with a tight fitting lid and remove from the heat. When you are ready to serve, continue from this point onwards - heat up the rice and broth and cook on from here.

4. Baked Leeks With Chevre, Proscuitto, And Mustard Champagne Dressing

Serving: Serves 10 | Prep: | Cook: | Ready in:

Ingredients

- 5 small leeks
- 6 ounces goat cheese
- 10 thin slices of proscuitto
- salt and pepper to taste
- 2 tablespoons whole ground mustard
- 2 ounces champagne (or white wine)

Direction

- Preheat oven to 400 degrees.
- For the leeks, boil 8 cups of water in a large pot with a palm-full of salt. Meanwhile, trim off green tops and reserve for your next pot of chicken stock. Trim the white end as closely to the root as possible, basically brushing your knife against the roots. You'll want your leeks to hold together, so if you trim too far up, they'll unravel, so-to-speak. Cut leeks in half lengthwise and wash well in cold water. Place leeks in boiling water and let cook for 5-6 minutes, or until the leeks are softened. Drain in a colander and run cold water over the leeks to stop them from cooking further.
- To assemble, take a leek half and pat dry with a kitchen towel. Peel back half the leaves from the green end of the leek, being careful not to peel too far back so to break the root end. Crumble about 1 Tbsp. of goat cheese on the exposed, inner leaf and fold outer leaves over cheese. At this point, you should have a leek and goat cheese sandwich (with the root end still attached). Repeat with the remaining leek halves.
- Wrap each leek in a piece of prosciutto and place side by side on a pan or in an oven-proof casserole dish.
- Once all the leeks have been wrapped, season with salt and pepper. Bake for 10-12 minutes, or until prosciutto is golden and cheese has melted.
- While leeks are baking, whisk mustard and champagne together. Spoon over leeks before serving.

5. Beef Braised With Pears And Champagne

Serving: Makes 6 servings | Prep: | Cook: | Ready in:

Ingredients

- 2 pounds chuck cut in one large chunk, tied
- 3 tablespoons safflower oil
- 1 medium-sized onion, finely chopped
- 1 small green bell pepper, finely chopped
- 2 stalks celery (the young, white part) finely chopped
- 4 firm but ripe pears, peeled, cored and cut into chunks
- a bouquet garni containing 1 bay leaf, 6 white peppercorns and 12 crushed cardamom pods
- 3 cups champagne (Gruet Sparkling from New Mexico is tasty and inexpensive.)
- 1 cup concentrated brown stock
- sea salt to taste

Direction

- Preheat oven to 425 degrees F. Brush the tied piece of beef with safflower oil and sear on all sides in a sauté pan. Set aside.
- Meanwhile, make a mirepoix of the chopped vegetables, and (using the same pan in which you seared the beef) sweat for about 10 minutes over medium low heat until the onion is translucent. Transfer mirepoix to an ovenproof casserole. Add the beef along with the pears, bouquet garni, 1 1/2 cups champagne and the brown stock.
- Cover the casserole with a sheet of aluminum foil, and place the lid atop the foil to seal the casserole. Place in the preheated oven. After 15 minutes, reduce the heat to 350 degrees F. Braise in the oven for 1 1/2 hours.
- Turn the meat in the liquid, add salt to taste and braise for another hour or until a sharp pronged fork will go into the meat fairly easily. Remove meat from the casserole and keep warm on a covered platter in the turned-off oven.

- Strain the cooking liquid through a sieve, pressing on the pears to get as much of their flavor (and bulk) as possible. Put the strained liquid into a medium sized saucepan and reduce the liquid until only about 3/4 cup remains. It should be a thick syrup. Set the pears aside.
- Finish the sauce by adding 1-1/2 cups champagne to the reduced syrup. Blend well and heat thoroughly.
- Slice the meat into 1/2-inch thick slices and plate with a spoonful of the cooked pears. Nap with the champagne sauce. Serve with scallion mashed potatoes and broccoli. Accompany by my favorite St. Julien, Ducru-Beaucaillou, or St. Supéry's Élu, a Bordeaux blend from Napa Valley -- or you could drink Champagne, if you like.

6. Beets Mimosa

Serving: Serves 4 | Prep: | Cook: | Ready in:

Ingredients

- For the roasted beets
- 4 beets, with fresh tops removed and saved
- Olive oil
- Kosher salt
- fresh ground black pepper
- a handful of fresh thyme
- For the beet stems:
- 1 cup beet stems, chopped fine
- 1/2 cup shallots, chopped fine
- 3/4 cup dry white wine
- 1/4 cup champagne vinegar
- 1 tablespoon balsamic vinegar
- 1 1/2 tablespoons walnut oil
- 2 teaspoons Italian parsley, minced
- 1 teaspoon tarragon, minced
- Kosher salt and fresh ground pepper
- 4 hard boiled eggs
- salmon roe

Direction

- For the roasted beets
- Preheat the oven to 350. Place the beets in an ovenproof casserole and drizzle them with olive oil and sprinkle them with salt and pepper. Spread the thyme across the top. Cover with foil. Place in the oven and bake for one hour. Some beets take longer to cook than others so at the one hour mark I test for doneness by inserting a toothpick into the largest beet. It should pierce easily until you get close to the middle. Then it should firm up. Don't worry by the time they cool there will be plenty of carry over cooking. If they are to firm place them back in the oven for 15 to 20 minutes. Remove them from the oven and let cool.
- For the beet stems:
- Place the beet stems, shallots, white wine into a medium sized sauté pan and place them over medium heat. Once they start to boil lower the heat and simmer until the wine is gone with the exception of a few bubbles. Add the champagne vinegar and reduce to a glaze. Add the balsamic, stir and remove from the heat. Let it cool to room temperature. Place the stem mixture in a mixing bowl and add the walnut oil, tarragon and parsley. Season with salt and pepper.
- Using a coarse strainer set over a mixing bowl smash the eggs through the mesh with the back of a spoon. Scrape the back of the strainer because a lot of eggy goodness will be hanging out there. Cut each beet into two 1/2 inch slices. Place on a cutting board and cut into rounds using a 2 inch diameter round cookie cutter. You want to have 8 rounds when finished. Season them with a touch of salt and a little pepper. Place the cookie cutter onto the center of a plate. Spoon a tablespoon of the beet stem mixture into the cutter spreading the mixture to the sides. Place a beet round on top and gently push down. Repeat one more time and remove the cutter by holding the top beet with a finger and lifting the cutter. Spoon a good sized portion of egg onto the top and

garnish with a small spoonful of salmon roe. Repeat this process with the remaining 3 plates. Serve.

7. Bette À Carde "Cymbeline"

Serving: Serves 4 | Prep: | Cook: | Ready in:

Ingredients

- 1 bunch bette à carde
- 1 cup flat Champagne (or verjus)
- Pinch sal de mer

Direction

- Wash bette à carde. Cut out midribs. If serving guests, feed midribs to goat. Otherwise, chop in small pieces.
- Chop leaves roughly.
- Simmer leaves (and optional midribs) in salted water till desired softness.
- Drain. Return to pot and add flat Champagne (or verjus). Cook one minute. Turn off heat and cover. Allow a short rest before serving.

8. Blackberry Brandy Slush

Serving: Serves 12 | Prep: 0hours10mins | Cook: 24hours0mins | Ready in:

Ingredients

- 2 cups Blackberry Brandy
- 1   can of lemonade concentrate
- 1   can orange juice concentrate
- 1 cup Sugar
- Moscato, champagne or Sprite to mix

Direction

- Add the brandy, two concentrates and sugar into a Tupperware-like container with a lid.

- Fill up an empty concentrate can with water six times and add that in.
- Stir it all up, pop a lid on and put it in the freezer.
- Let it freeze for 24-48 hours, stirring a few times (I stirred twice and served it at the 24-hour mark). The sugar really sinks to the bottom, so keep that in mind when you mix.
- When you're ready to serve, fill your glass up about 2/3 with slush and mix in Moscato, champagne or Sprite/7-up the remainder of the way.

9. Blackberry Champagne Cocktail

Serving: Serves 6 | Prep: | Cook: | Ready in:

Ingredients

- 1/2 cup Brandy
- 4 1/2 teaspoons sugar
- 1 pint blackberries
- 750 milliliters brut Champagne
- 750 milliliters Lindeman's Framboise

Direction

- 1. Stir sugar and brandy in medium bowl. Crush about 10 blackberries; add to brandy mixture. Let stand 1 hour at room temperature, then strain. (Can be prepared 1 day ahead. Cover; chill brandy mixture and remaining blackberries separately.)
- 2. Divide brandy mixture among 6 Champagne glasses. Add 2 blackberries to each glass. Fill halfway with Framboise and the rest of the way with Champagne; serve.

10. Blood Orange Fennel Salad

Serving: Serves 2 | Prep: | Cook: | Ready in:

Ingredients

- Salad:
- 1   small fennel bulb
- 3   small blood oranges
- 2   cups boiling water
- 1/2   lemon
- 1 teaspoon fresh rosemary leaves
- Dressing:
- 2 tablespoons Orange Champagne Vinegar (TJ's)
- 1 teaspoon champagne vinegar
- 1 teaspoon white vinegar
- 1 teaspoon ground coriander
- 1 teaspoon walnut oil

Direction

- Put the 2 cups of hot water into a medium sized bowl, adding the juice of 1/2 the lemon. Slice the fennel bulb into thin strips and rounds. Place the sliced fennel into the bowl of lemon water and let sit for 5 minutes, making sure they're all submerged.
- While the fennel is in the water, peel the 3 blood oranges and take off as much white pith as you can. Keeping the oranges whole, slice them into ¼" thick rounds. Some of them will break depending on the juiciness of the orange, but now you've got some variation in your salad!
- Mix the vinegars and oil together and add the coriander. This dressing needs no salt as the sweetness in the orange juice and the acid in the vinegars make a pretty complete dressing. I used about 4 short rosemary stalks to get the leaves.
- It's best to compose this salad into individual plates. Drain the fennel and alternate layering the oranges and fennel onto each plate, spooning the dressing between each layer. Sprinkle the fresh rosemary over the salad.
- P.s. If you don't have TJ orange champagne vinegar, making its replacement is not too difficult. Substitute the champagne vinegar with apple cider and white wine vinegar and add 2 tablespoons of orange juice. When I ran out of my last TJ's bottle and after realizing how much it cost (I loved it so much I never looked) I swore I'd be making my own version and because I'm such a huge fan of Marshall's I was rewarded by finding a bottle of standalone champagne vinegar in their gourmet food shelves during the holiday season. I was one psyched cook!!!!

11. Blue Skies

Serving: Serves 1 | Prep: | Cook: | Ready in:

Ingredients

- 1/2 ounce Blue Curacao
- 1/2 ounce Amaretto
- 1/2 ounce Champagne
- 1/2 ounce Lemon Juice

Direction

- Pour the Blue Curacao, Amaretto and Lemon Juice into a champagne flute and stir well.
- Top off with the Champagne, stir lightly and serve.

12. Bourbon Presse

Serving: Makes 1 drink | Prep: | Cook: | Ready in:

Ingredients

- 1 shot Good bourbon - quality matters here
- 2 ounces Freshly-squeezed orange juice
- 2 ounces Freshly-squeezed lemon juice
- Dry champagne or sparkling wine
- Lemon and/or orange round (optional)

Direction

- Fill a highball glass halfway with cubed ice.
- Add first three ingredients and stir.
- Top with sparkling wine or champagne; garnish with lemon/orange round if using.

- Enjoy outside in the sunshine, if possible, accompanied by good friends or some quality reading material.

13. Caesar Bread Salad Or Panzanella Giulio

Serving: Serves 4 | Prep: | Cook: |Ready in:

Ingredients

- Dressing
- juice of one lemon
- 1 teaspoon champagne vinegar
- 2 teaspoons dijon mustard
- 2 cloves garlic
- 1 teaspoon Worcestershire sauce
- dash Tabasco sauce
- 2 anchovy filets, minced (may be omitted)
- 1 egg, room temperature
- 1/2 cup olive oil
- pepper, salt to taste
- 1/2 cup grated aged parmesan
- Salad
- 1 loaf (16. oz) day-old Italian bread, crust removed or intact
- 1 head Romaine lettuce
- 1 avocado, cubed
- 1/2 English cucumber
- 1 lb. fresh asparagus, chopped into bite size pieces on the diagonal

Direction

- Fill medium sized pot with water and bring to a boil. Place egg in small heat resistant container and pour over boiling water. Let sit for 1 minute. Then, carefully remove egg from water and set aside. Reserve the rest of the water for later.
- Whisk together lemon juice, champagne vinegar, Dijon mustard, garlic, Worcestershire sauce, Tabasco sauce, and minced anchovy filets in large glass bowl. Then lightly whisk in egg. The white will be runny and the yolk slightly thicker than normal.
- Begin adding oil drop by drop and whisking at the same time. As emulsion begins to take continue whisking and increase rate of oil to thin stream. When you have added all of the oil the dressing will be thin and slightly yellow.
- Salt and pepper to taste and add grated parmesan. Set dressing aside.
- Cut bread into one-inch cubes. Day-old bread will soak up the dressing better, but fresh bread will work also. I prefer to leave the crust because it adds a nice chewy texture to the salad. Remove, wash, and chop Romaine into bite-size pieces. Combine dressing, bread, and lettuce in large bowl and let sit in the refrigerator for 30 minutes to allow the dressing to soak in.
- At this point, bring water back to boil and parboil asparagus for two minutes, until it is cooked, but still crunchy. Then, plunge asparagus into ice bath to cool down. Cut avocado and cucumber into 1/2 inch cubes. When bread, lettuce and dressing have taken their half hour time-out in the fridge, combine with the rest of your ingredients and serve immediately with more sliced parmesan on top if you desire. Pairs well with fruity white wines!

14. Carey Nershi's Angostura Sugar Cubes For Champagne Cocktails

Serving: Makes about a pint jar's worth of sugar cubes for many champagne cocktails | Prep: | Cook: |Ready in:

Ingredients

- 1 cup superfine sugar (see note above)
- 1 tablespoon (1/2 fluid ounce) Angostura bitters

- Champagne or sparkling wine for serving
- Lemon twists for serving (optional)

Direction

- Combine sugar and bitters in a bowl and stir until liquid is evenly distributed. Use your fingers to pinch the mixture if needed, to make the mixture uniformly pink.
- If using molds, press the mixture into molds, packing it down as much as possible. Microwave at 50% power for 20 to 30 seconds. Alternatively, you can let the molds sit out overnight to dry and harden. Once set, pop the cubes out of the mold.
- If not using molds, heat the oven to 250° F and line an oven-safe baking pan with parchment paper. (The cubes were made in a standard 9- x 5-inch loaf pan.)
- Pour the sugar onto the parchment paper. Pack the sugar into the base of the pan very tightly with a spatula, meat pounder, or another tool that is stiff and flat. The height should be similar to a commercial sugar cube, around 1.27cm/1/2 inch.
- Using a thin knife, score the sugar into a grid of cubes of the size you want, slicing all the way through the layer of sugar. Put the pan in the oven to dry for 1 hour.
- Remove the pan of sugar from the oven and let the sugar cubes cool for at least 10 minutes.
- Break up the cubes. Pull the sugar cubes out of the pan and break them apart with your hands or something smooth and sturdy like a table knife or bench scraper. If cut properly, they will break fairly easy.
- Store the sugar cubes in an airtight container. To serve, put a sugar cube in a coupe glass or Champagne flute and pour Champagne or sparkling wine over. Garnish with a lemon twist if you like.

15. Cauliflower Steaks With Olive Salsa And Roasted Tomato Sauce

Serving: Serves 2 | Prep: 30hours0mins | Cook: 1hours0mins |Ready in:

Ingredients

- 1   large head cauliflower
- 4   vine ripe tomatoes
- 1   yellow onion
- 5   cloves of garlic, peeled
- 1/4 cup pitted green olives, diced
- 1/3 cup chopped cilantro
- 2 tablespoons champagne vinegar
- 1 tablespoon Mike's hot honey
- olive oil
- salt & pepper

Direction

- Preheat oven to 400°. Remove leaves and trim the end of the cauliflower. Cut into four 1/2" steaks from the center of the cauliflower. Reserve the small florets that break loose, and break into small pieces. Season cauliflower with the salt and pepper (and a dash of paprika and cumin if you'd like). Place seasoned cauliflower onto a baking sheet and drizzle with olive oil, and roast in the oven for about 30 minutes, flipping once, until crispy around the edges.
- Quarter the tomatoes and place them onto a rimmed baking sheet with the garlic cloves. Halve the onion (reserve one half) and quarter one half. Break apart and scatter the onions in the baking dish with the tomatoes and garlic. Drizzle everything with olive oil, season with salt and pepper, and roast in the oven for 30 minutes as well, stirring as needed. Once done, remove from oven and transfer to a heated skillet with a bit of olive oil. While sautéing, mash up the garlic, tomatoes, and onions with a wooden spoon, leaving it chunky. Allow it to reduce a bit, then remove

from the heat. Toss in 1 tbsp. of the chopped cilantro, and add salt and pepper to taste.
- While everything is in the oven, make the relish. Finely dice the remaining half an onion, and place in a bowl with the reserved cauliflower bits, chopped olives, cilantro, champagne vinegar, and Mike's hot honey. Mash everything together until it's incorporated.
- To assemble, spread the tomato sauce onto each plate, then place the cauliflower on top. Garnish with olive salsa, and serve while still warm.

16. Champagne Broiled Mangoes With Cookie Butter

Serving: Serves 4 | Prep: | Cook: |Ready in:

Ingredients

- Champagne Broiled Mangoes
- 3 Large, ripe mangoes, peeled and cubed (you want 2.5 to 3 cups)
- 1 1/4 cups Champagne, divided
- Zest and juice of 1 lime
- 2 tablespoons Chopped mint leaves
- 3 tablespoons Sugar
- 1 1/2 tablespoons Pomegranate molasses
- 1/4 teaspoon Ground ginger
- 1 cup Freshly whipped cream, unsweetened
- Homemade cookie butter (recipe below)
- Homemade Cookie Butter
- 5 1/4 to 5 1/2 ounces of crisp, thin ginger cookies (I use one sleeve of Anna's brand ginger thins). You want a crisp, not a soft or chewy, style cookie
- 1/2 teaspoon Ground cinnamon
- 1/8 teaspoon Ground nutmeg
- 1/8 teaspoon Ground cloves
- 1 tablespoon Sugar
- Pinch of sea or kosher salt
- 3 tablespoons Coconut oil
- 2 tablespoons Whole milk

Direction

- Champagne Broiled Mangoes
- In an ovenproof baking dish or glass pie dish, combine the cubed mango, 1/4 cup of the champagne, the lime juice and zest and the chopped mint leaves. Stir to combine. Set aside to marinate for thirty minutes.
- Preheat your broiler to high. I position my oven rack one rung down from the closest to the broiler so the mango has a few caramelized spots but isn't too charred, and the mint doesn't burn.
- Place the mango under the broiler for five minutes, stir, then broil for another three to four minutes. Watch carefully during the last few minutes of broiling. Remove and let cool for a few minutes - you want to serve the mango warm, not scorching.
- I like to start the champagne reduction as soon as I put the mango in to broil - that way it's done when the mango is ready to serve. In a small non-reactive saucepan, heat the remaining cup of champagne, the sugar and the pomegranate molasses over medium heat. Simmer until reduced by 3/4 and syrupy - about 15 minutes. Remove from heat and sprinkle the ground ginger in. Stir to combine. Note: if you make this before the mango, and it has time to completely cool, it may become quite thick and not easy to pour/drizzle. No worries - when you are ready to serve, just warm over low heat for a few minutes.
- Divide the broiled mango between four serving dishes (or martini glasses, if you'd like to be fancy). Drizzle each with a spoonful of the champagne reduction (not too much - it packs a punch). Top each with a dollop of whipped cream and then a small spoonful of the cookie butter. To finish, drizzle a bit more champagne reduction over the top.
- Homemade Cookie Butter
- Pulverize the cookies in a food processor until powdery and no large chunks remain. Sprinkle the cinnamon, nutmeg, cloves, sugar and salt into the crumbled cookies and pulse several times to combine.

- Add the coconut oil. Note: you want the coconut oil liquefied - if it is solid, warm it in the microwave for a few seconds at a time until it liquefies. Make sure it is not hot though when you add it to the cookie crumbs. Pulse until the coconut oil is incorporated into the cookie crumbs. It should look like wet sand at this point.
- Remove the mixture from the food processor into a mixing bowl. Gently stir in the milk, one tablespoon at a time (don't do this step in the food processor - over processing can turn the mixture clumpy and gummy.) The "butter" will look and feel like a very dense nut butter and it will hold together - won't be crumbly - this is what you want.
- Cover and leave at room temperature if you will be using shortly. If you make the day before, cover and refrigerate. It will harden up in the fridge, so allow it time to come to room temperature before using. Note: this recipe makes more than you need for the mango dessert, but in my opinion, that's great news for my breakfast toast! To store the leftovers, do as mentioned above - store in fridge and allow to warm up before using.

17. Champagne Ganache

Serving: Makes 3 cups | Prep: | Cook: | Ready in:

Ingredients

- 1 tablespoon Powdered gelatin
- 3 tablespoons Cold water
- 2/3 cup Champagne or sparkling wine
- 2 tablespoons Cognac or other brandy
- 1/2 teaspoon Vanilla extract
- 1/4 cup Heavy cream
- 3 tablespoons Light corn syrup
- 2 cups 38% Milk chocolate chips, feves, or chopped 38% milk chocolate, melted
- 2 ounces 61% bittersweet chocolate, chopped and melted
- 9 tablespoons Unsalted butter, softened

Direction

- Sprinkle the gelatin over the cold water in a small bowl. Let sit for 10 minutes, until the gelatin softens.
- Meanwhile, pour the Champagne, Cognac, and vanilla into a measuring cup.
- Combine the melted chocolates in a medium bowl. Combine the cream, softened gelatin, and corn syrup and pour over the chocolates and, using a small silicone spatula, stir the mixture in one direction, concentrating on the center, until the ganache is smooth and glistening.
- Slowly pour the Champagne into the ganache, whisking constantly (if you add the Champagne too quickly, the ganache will separate). Add the butter and stir until it is completely melted, about 1 minute. Put the ganache in the coolest part of your kitchen and let set, stirring occasionally, until spreadable, for about 1 hour before using.
- Leftover ganache can be covered and refrigerated for up to 2 weeks.

18. Champagne Grape Pizza With Asparagus

Serving: Makes 1 small pizza | Prep: | Cook: | Ready in:

Ingredients

- Champagne Soaked Grapes
- 3.5 cups grapes
- 2 cups champagne
- Grape and Asparagus Pizza
- 1/2 serving pizza dough, store bought or homemade
- 1 handful champagne soaked grapes
- 5 pieces asparagus spears, ends cut off
- 1 handful shredded cheese, mozzarella preferred
- 1 teaspoon olive oil

Direction

- Champagne Soaked Grapes
- Cut the grapes in half.
- Pour the champagne over the grapes and let soak overnight.
- Grape and Asparagus Pizza
- Preheat oven to 425 degrees.
- Make or buy pizza dough and cut it in half to form your own personal pizza.
- Slather dough with olive oil.
- Top dough with cheese, grapes, and asparagus.
- Season with salt and pepper.
- Bake in a 425 oven for 15 minutes or until bubbly, golden hot.
- Eat with a side of grape flavored champagne.

19. Champagne Marshmallow Treats

Serving: Makes 8 to 10 treats | Prep: | Cook: | Ready in:

Ingredients

- 6 tablespoons (85 g) unsalted butter
- 1/4 cup (59 ml) dry champagne
- 6 cups (318 g) mini marshmallows
- 1/2 teaspoon vanilla extract
- 1/4 teaspoon kosher salt
- 6 cups (192 g) crisped rice cereal

Direction

- Line a 9 x 9-inch (23 x 23-cm) baking dish with foil. Spray with non-stick cooking spray and set it aside.
- In a large skillet preheated to medium heat, melt the butter. Add the champagne, stir and let it simmer for about minute. Next, add the marshmallows, vanilla extract and kosher salt. Stir the marshmallows until completely melted, or about 4 minutes.
- Remove the skillet from the heat and add-in the cereal. Stir to combine. Pour the mixture into the prepared baking dish. Press the

mixture into the dish and let it cool completely before slicing it and serving!
- Variation: Throw caution to the wind and try these treats with rosé or white wine!

20. Champagne Oysters

Serving: Serves 6 | Prep: | Cook: | Ready in:

Ingredients

- 12 pieces Oysters
- 3 ounces Unsalted Butter
- 1 1/2 cups Brut Champagne
- 3 tablespoons Chives, minced
- 1 teaspoon sea salt
- Rock Salt

Direction

- Preheat your oven to 400 degrees. Shucking oysters is something that does require finesse. Buy them only from a reputable seafood purveyor, who you trust to only sell fresh oysters. If possible, get that person to shuck the oysters for you. However, it isn't impossible to do it yourself.
- If you are right handed (opposite true for lefties), place a thick dishtowel in the center of your left hand, and place the hinge of one oyster into the palm of the towel wielding hand. If you don't have an oyster knife in your crappy little kitchen, not to worry. Take a butter knife (not a paring knife – you will cut yourself!), and insert the tip between the 2 shells against the little protrusion, and while applying firm pressure, wiggle the blade between the shells. Once the shells are pried apart, take your paring knife and carefully separate the top shell from the bottom one holding the oyster. Run the knife along the bottom shell, cutting through the two muscles and free the oyster, but leave it in the shell. Repeat with the remaining 11 oysters.

- While you wait for the liquid to reduce, place the oysters on the half shell on a baking sheet. If they are rounded enough that they might tip over, put a small pile of rock salt under each shell to keep them level. Put the oysters in the oven and roast for 5 minutes. When you take them out of the oven be careful not to lose any of the juice inside the shells.
- Turn the heat on your reduced Champagne down to low. Slowly (a tablespoon at a time) whisk the butter into the reduced Champagne. Whisk quickly in order to emulsify the butter and Champagne, and remove from the heat. Season to your taste with salt.
- Fill a serving tray with rock salt and arrange the oysters on top. Spoon about a teaspoon of Champagne butter sauce over each oyster on the half shell, and top with a strip of chive at an angle over the oyster like a sword. Serve immediately.

21. Champagne Poached Pear Cheesecake With Pistachio Crust

Serving: Serves 8 | Prep: | Cook: | Ready in:

Ingredients

- For the pear topping
- 1 cup Extra dry champagne
- 1/3 cup Sugar
- 1/4 cup Water
- 1 Vanilla bean, halved lengthwise
- 2 Firm, ripe pears, peeled, cored, and halved
- 5 Cardamom pods
- For the cheesecake
- 1 cup Shelled pistachios
- 1 1/2 teaspoons Orange zest
- 1/8 teaspoon Kosher salt
- 1 teaspoon Ground cinnamon
- 5 tablespoons Sugar
- 4 tablespoons Unsalted Butter, melted
- 4 8 oz. Packages cream cheese, softened
- 1 cup Sour cream
- 1 cup Sugar
- 1 teaspoon Pure vanilla extract
- 1 teaspoon Ground cardamom
- 1 Egg, slightly beaten
- 1 tablespoon All purpose flour

Direction

- In a large skillet, combine the champagne, sugar, water, vanilla bean and cardamom pods. Bring to a boil over medium high heat, stirring to dissolve sugar. Reduce heat. Add pears, cover and simmer 8-10 minutes until pears are just tender. Remove from heat. Drain pears, discard liquid and spices. Transfer to a bowl, cover and chill for at least an hour.
- Preheat oven to 325 degrees. Place pistachios, orange zest, salt, cinnamon, and sugar in a food processor. Pulse until nuts are ground. Add the melted butter and pulse 2-3 times just until combined. Press mixture into the bottom of a 9" spring form pan. Bake for 10-12 minutes just until it starts to brown. Remove from oven and set aside to cool.
- In a large mixing bowl combine the cream cheese, Sour cream, sugar, vanilla and cardamom. Cream ingredients together until well combined. Add the egg and flour. Mix just until evenly distributed. Don't over mix. Pour cream cheese mixture into the spring form pan with the prepared crust. Bake for 60 minutes. (I recommend using the water bath method.) Leave the cheesecake in the oven, but turn the oven off and crack open the door. Allow oven to cool completely. Remove the cake from the oven, cover with plastic wrap and refrigerate for at least 1 hour.
- Just before serving, slice the pears lengthwise into 1/4 - 3/8" wide slices. Arrange the pears in a circular fan design on top of the cake.

22. Champagne Pork Chops

Serving: Serves 4 | Prep: | Cook: | Ready in:

Ingredients

- 4 Pork Chops, bone in, about 1 inch thick
- 3/4 cup Champagne Vinegar
- 1/2 cup Chicken Stock or Broth
- 1 tablespoon Honey
- 2 Sage Leaves
- 2 tablespoons Grapeseed Oil (or Canola Oil)
- 3/4 cup Shallots, thinly sliced
- 2 Cloves Garlic, minced or pressed
- 3/4 cup Champagne or Sparkling Wine
- 1/2 teaspoon Ground Coriander
- 1 teaspoon Whole Grain Dijon Mustard
- 1/3 cup Creme Fraiche
- 1 tablespoon Chives, chopped
- 1 tablespoon Parsley, chopped
- Salt & Pepper

Direction

- Salt each pork chop with 1 teaspoon salt each and place on a wire rack set on top of a baking sheet. Let stand unrefrigerated for at least 45 minutes.
- Meanwhile, in a small saucepan, bring the champagne vinegar, chicken stock, sage leaves, and honey to a boil. Reduce heat and simmer until reduced to 1/2 cup - approximately 25-30 minutes. Remove sage leaves and set aside the reduced mixture.
- Preheat oven to 275 degrees. Put the baking sheet/wire rack in the oven and cook the pork chops until a thermometer inserted into the center of the chop registers 115 degrees, approximately 25-30 minutes. Remove from oven.
- Place a large skillet with grapeseed oil over high heat until smoking. Sear the chops until golden on each side about 2-3 minutes per side. Then stand up and sear the non-bone edge. Remove the pork chops to a plate once cooked through to your liking and loosely tent with foil [Note: if you can't fit all 4 pork chops in one skillet, do not crowd - simply cook in two batches using 1 TB oil for each batch.
- There should be about 1 TB oil remaining in the pan. You can add additional grapeseed oil

if necessary to reach approximately 1 TB. Turn the heat down to medium high and add the shallots, garlic, and a sprinkle of salt and saute until golden. Reduce heat to medium and deglaze the pan with the champagne and let it reduce down. Then add the reduced champagne vinegar mixture, the coriander, and the mustard and let it reduce for a few minutes. Add the creme fraiche and the chives and parsley. Let it cook for 1-2 minutes. Add salt and pepper to taste.

- Return the chops to the pan and quickly coat in the sauce. Plate each chop, topping with a generous scoop of shallots and sauce.
- If you didn't already finish off the champagne, enjoy the remainder with dessert or a nice piece of oozy cheese.

23. Champagne Punch Drink Recipe

Serving: Serves 2 | Prep: | Cook: | Ready in:

Ingredients

- 1 cup Frozen Lemonade
- 5 cups Frozen Strawberry Juice
- 3 cups Pine Apple Juice Frozen
- 1 cup Ginger Ale, Chilled
- 1 cup Champagne

Direction

- step1- Take a punch bowl and add the lemonade concentrate, strawberry juice, pineapple juice to itStep2 -Mix them well and stir the ingredients with ginger aleStep3 - Then add champagne to it at the end. Remember not to stir champagneStep4 - The Strawberry Champagne is ready to refresh you. Serve it at a bridal shower and for sure everyone loves it.

24. Champagne Rhubarb Jelly Shots

Serving: Makes 30 squares | Prep: | Cook: |Ready in:

Ingredients

- Rhubarb Syrup
- 1 pound rhubarb, cut into 1/4-inch pieces
- 1 cup lemon juice
- 1 cup water
- 2 cups sugar
- Rhubarb Jelly
- 2 cups rhubarb syrup, divided
- 8 packets powdered gelatin, like Knox
- 1 cup lemon juice
- 1/2 cup gin
- 1/4 cup sugar
- 3 cups champagne

Direction

- Rhubarb Syrup
- Combine all ingredients in a medium saucepan on medium-low heat and simmer for about an hour, or until liquid turns a bright ruby red and rhubarb has softened.
- Cool to room temperature, and strain through a mesh strainer.
- Rhubarb Jelly
- Wipe a 9 x 13-inch rectangular baking pan with about a teaspoon of vegetable oil. Heat 1 1/2 cups of the rhubarb syrup in a small saucepan, until it is hot but not boiling, and whisk in 2 packets of gelatin. Whisk for 2 to 3 minutes, and allow to cool slightly. Pour through a mesh strainer (to get out any lumps of gelatin) into the prepared baking pan, and refrigerate for about an hour, until solidified.
- Now heat 1 cup of lemon juice with remaining 1/2 cup of rhubarb syrup and 1/4 cup of sugar in a small saucepan, stirring until sugar is dissolved and mixture is hot but not boiling. Remove from heat and whisk in remaining 6 packets of gelatin, stirring for 2 to 3 minutes. Pour through a mesh strainer into a large mixing bowl. Whisk in gin, followed by champagne, and pour into baking pan, over the rhubarb layer. Refrigerate for 4 to 5 hours or overnight.
- Once the jelly has solidified, run a thin spatula around the edges to loosen it from the pan. Set a large cutting board over the top of the pan, and carefully invert, so that the jelly flips onto the cutting board in one big rectangle. Using a straight, sharp knife, cut jelly into 1-inch squares and refrigerate until ready to serve.

25. Champagne Risotto

Serving: Serves 4 as a first course, 6-8 as a side dish | Prep: | Cook: |Ready in:

Ingredients

- 1 quart Chicken stock
- 3 shallots, minced
- 1 clove garlic, minced
- 4 tablespoons unsalted butter, divided
- 1 tablespoon olive oil
- 1.5 cups Carnaroli or Arborio rice
- 1 cup Champagne or other sparkling wine
- .75 cups grated Parmesan
- 2 tablespoons heavy cream
- .25 teaspoons freshly ground pepper
- sea salt to taste
- shaved parmesan cheese (optional garnish)
- Splash white truffle oil (optional garnish)

Direction

- Bring the broth to a simmer in a medium saucepan and keep warm over low heat.
- Heat 2 Tbsp. butter and the olive oil in a separate medium saucepan over medium heat until the butter is melted.
- Add the shallots and garlic and cook until softened, but not brown, about 5 minutes.
- Stir in the rice and cook until it is well-coated with the oil/butter mixture and begins to turn translucent, about 1-2 minutes.
- Add the champagne and simmer until all of the liquid is absorbed, about 3-5 minutes.

- Add about 1 cup of the warm broth from to the rice and stir regularly until the liquid is absorbed, about 3-5 minutes. You'll know the liquid is absorbed when you run your spoon through the rice and liquid doesn't immediately fill the bottom of the pan. Repeat, adding broth 1 cup at a time, until the rice is al dente (cooked through but still firm), about 18-22 minutes. While you don't have to stir the rice the entire time, you shouldn't leave the rice unattended for more than a minute or two and do stir the rice frequently.
- Combine the Parmesan, heavy cream, and pepper in a bowl.
- When the risotto is done, remove the pan from the heat and stir in the cheese, cream, and pepper mixture long with the remaining 2 Tbsp. of butter. Add salt to taste. Garnish at will.

26. Champagne Three Citrus Sorbet

Serving: Makes 10 to 12 servings | Prep: | Cook: |Ready in:

Ingredients

- For the Sorbet
- • 4 cups good quality Champagne
- • 2 cups granulated sugar
- • 2 cups water
- • 2 cups freshly squeezed ruby-red grapefruit juice (5 to 6 grapefruits)
- • 2 cups freshly squeezed orange juice (7 to 8 oranges)
- • 1/2 cup freshly squeezed Meyer lemon juice (2 to 3 Meyer lemons)
- • 1/2 cup heavy cream or whole milk Greek-style yogurt (optional)
- For garnishes and citrus-honey caramel
- • 1 blood orange or Pink Navel orange
- • Confectioners' sugar for dusting
- • 2 ruby-red grapefruits
- • 1/4 cup freshly squeezed grapefruit juice + segments from 1 grapefruit
- • 1/4 cup freshly squeezed Meyer lemon juice
- • 2 tablespoons raw orange blossom honey
- • A few walnuts or any nuts of your choice

Direction

- For the Sorbet
- Open the champagne bottle 1 to 2 hours before using. Gradually pour champagne, allowing for foaming, into a 2-quart Picher; set aside.
- In a medium saucepan over medium-heat, heat sugar and water. Stir until mixture comes to a boil; reduce heat to low and simmer 5 minutes. Remove from heat, cover, and let stand until cooled. To the champagne add all of the juices with the pulp; stir until well blended.
- Ice Cream Maker method: Transfer mixture to ice cream maker and process according to manufacturer's instructions.
- Freezer method: Pour the sorbet mixture into shallow container, cover and place in the freezer. When it is almost solid, mash it up with a fork and freeze again. When frozen-solid, place in a blender, add the heavy cream or yogurt (if using) and process until smooth. Cover and freeze until ready to serve. Can be prepared 3 days in advance.
- For garnishes and citrus-honey caramel
- Preheat oven to 250 degrees F. Wash and dry the blood orange; then slice off thin rounds. Arrange on a baking sheet lined with parchment paper or nonstick baking mat; liberally dust each round with confectioners' sugar. Cook until completely dry, flipping and dusting some more with confectioners' sugar, about 45 minutes to 1 hour or more.
- To make the broiled grapefruit baskets for serving: Heat broiler, place the oven rack about 6 inches from heat. Halve grapefruits and carefully cut out the segments and then membranes with a small sharp knife, trying not to piers the grapefruit halves. Sprinkle the insides of each half with confectioners' sugar. Broil until browned in spots on top, 3 to 5 minutes.

- To make the honey-citrus caramel: In a small saucepan combine the juices and honey and cook over medium-low heat until it starts to boil; then turn-down the heat to low and simmer, swirling the pan occasionally, until thickened and large bubbles appear.
- Meanwhile arrange the grapefruit segments and nuts on a plate. Slightly cool the caramel and then pour over the segments and nuts. Place in refrigerator to chill until ready to serve.

27. Champagne Raspberry Heart Shaped Cake With Cream Cheese Brown Sugar Frosting

Serving: Makes 1 cake | Prep: | Cook: | Ready in:

Ingredients

- For the Cake
- 1 8 inch square pan, greased and floured
- 1 8 inch round cake pan, greased and floured
- 2 cups cake flour
- 2 teaspoons baking powder
- 1/4 teaspoon baking soda
- 1/4 teaspoon salt
- 1 cup sugar
- 1 cup oil
- 1/2 cup buttermilk
- 3 eggs
- 3/4 cup champagne
- 2 tablespoons raspberry liquor
- 1 teaspoon vanilla
- Cream cheese brown sugar frosting
- 2 8 oz packages cream cheese softened
- 1 stick butter softened
- 1/2 cup sour cream
- 1/2 cup brown sugar
- 1 teaspoon vanilla
- 1 tablespoon raspberry liquor
- 2 drops red food coloring
- 3 cups confectioner's sugar

Direction

- Preheat the oven to 350
- Sift together cake flour, baking powder, baking soda and salt in a medium bowl
- In a large mixing bowl, whisk the sugar and oil until well blended.
- Whisk in the buttermilk, then add the eggs one at a time
- Whisk in the champagne, liquor and vanilla, then slowly whisk in the dry ingredients, do not over whisk, lumps are ok
- Divide batter so both cakes are at the same level and bake until golden brown or until cake tester or toothpick comes out clean, about 25 minutes
- Allow to cool completely before frosting
- To make the frosting, beat cream cheese, butter, sour cream and brown sugar until fluffy, about 2-3 minutes
- Add vanilla and liquor
- Slowly add confectioner's sugar until well combined, then add the food coloring and beat on high speed for another minute for a very light frosting
- To assemble the cake, using either a piece of cardboard covered with foil or a very large baking pan, gently invert both cakes from the pan.
- Cut the circle in half, placing one half on consecutive sides of the square
- Use a small amount of frosting to make a crumb layer, then generously frost the entire cake.
- Allow to chill and serve.

28. Cheese Ball With Pecans And Dried Cranberries

Serving: Makes 4 large cheese balls | Prep: | Cook: | Ready in:

Ingredients

- 2 teaspoons extra-virgin olive oil

- 3 to 5 large shallots, finely chopped (about 1/2 cup)
- 4 cloves garlic, peeled and grated or finely chopped
- 1 teaspoon creamy Dijon mustard
- 2 tablespoons apricot jam (any large chunks removed or chopped up)
- 2 teaspoons Worcestershire sauce
- 1 teaspoon lemon zest
- 1 tablespoon lemon juice
- 1 teaspoon Champagne vinegar
- 1 tablespoon Sriracha (or Tabasco), more to taste
- 1 teaspoon kosher salt
- 4 tablespoons unsalted butter, room temperature
- 8 ounces cream cheese, room temperature
- 2 tablespoons mayonnaise
- 5 cups grated cheddar cheddar (I recommend a combination of mellow and sharp)
- 1/2 cup creamy blue cheese (I use Mountain Gorgonzola)
- 1/2 cup pecans, chopped
- 1/3 cup dried sweetened cranberries, chopped
- 2 tablespoons fig jam

Direction

- Turn heat to medium under a medium-sized frying pan. Add olive oil. When the oil is hot and shimmery, add the shallots. Cook until they soften and just start to get crispy (about 10 minutes). Turn to low heat and add the garlic. Cook for one minute. Turn off the heat and stir in mustard, apricot jam, Worcestershire sauce, lemon zest, lemon juice, Champagne vinegar, hot sauce, and salt. Set aside.
- Place butter and cream cheese in a standing mixer bowl. With the paddle attachment, whip until smooth and light (about 2 minutes). Scrape down the sides. Add mayonnaise, cheddar, and blue cheese. Whip again on medium for about 30 seconds. Scrape down the side. Add shallot/garlic mixture. Mix for another 30 seconds. Taste. Adjust. It might

need more salt. Add more Sriracha if it doesn't have enough kick. And often, I need to add some acid (more lemon juice or vinegar). Mix well after adjusting the balance.

- At this point, you should chill the mixture so it's easier to handle. Or go for it and just brave the sticky mess. The thing to remember is you will be rolling it in nuts and dried fruit so it doesn't have to be perfect looking. After an hour or so in the fridge, use saran wrap to shape the mixture into any size balls and/or logs. Chill in the fridge for a few hours or overnight. Or freeze for a few months.
- Take the cheese balls out of the fridge about 30 minutes before serving it (a few hours before if frozen). Place chopped nuts and cranberries on a large plate. Use your hands (fun!) to cover the ball with a thin and even coating of fig jam. Place cheese ball on nut/cranberry plate. Wash your hands. Then go to town rolling the ball in the pecans and cranberries. You might need to use your hands a bit to make sure the goodies stick. Serve immediately with classic round butter crackers.

29. Chicken Salad With Cornichons And Radishes

Serving: Serves four | Prep: | Cook: |Ready in:

Ingredients

- 2-3 cups pulled roasted chicken
- 2 eggs
- 1 cup radishes, julienned
- 1/2 cup cornichons, chopped
- 2 tablespoons Champagne or white wine vinegar
- 1/2 cup Good {translation: full fat} mayonnaise
- 1/4 cup finely chopped chives
- A little fresh taragon (chopped) to garnish
- 1 Large sheet Lavash flatbread {optional}
- Olive oil {optional}

- Kosher salt & pepper

Direction

- In a small sauce pan, bring about 3 cups of water to a boil. Gently roll in the eggs with a spoon and let boil for 15 minutes. Once the timer goes off, plunge the eggs into an ice water bath. Set aside.
- In a mixing bowl, toss the pulled chicken breast, radishes, and cornichons. In a small bowl, whisk the mayonnaise and champagne vinegar together. Add the mixture to the larger bowl and toss the ingredients together so that everything is evenly coated.
- Once the eggs have cooled, remove the shells and chop. Gently fold them into the chicken salad. Season with salt and pepper to taste and a little finely chopped fresh tarragon to taste.
- If not serving with toast or sliced bread, preheat the oven to about 375 degrees. Place the sheet of Lavash on a baking sheet, and lightly brush each side with olive oil and a sprinkling of kosher salt. Bake on each side for four minutes.
- Once the Lavash is golden brown, cut it into squares and serve with the chicken salad.

30. Chocolate Pasta Napolean With Raspberry Coulis And Whipped Cream

Serving: Serves 4 | Prep: | Cook: | Ready in:

Ingredients

- Raspberry Coulis and Raspberry Whipped Cream
- 1 cup Heavy Whipping Cream
- 1.25 cups Raspberries
- Sugar to Taste
- 1 splash Champagne Vinegar
- Chocolate Pasta
- 2 cups All purpose flour
- 2 egg (about 4 oz total)

- 3 tablespoons Cocoa Powder
- 2 tablespoons Sugar
- 1 pinch Salt

Direction

- Raspberry Coulis and Raspberry Whipped Cream
- Add Raspberries to Blender/Vitamix and blend completely. Check sweetness and add sugar to taste (I added about 2 Tablespoons) and blend to combine.
- Strain thoroughly using a fine mesh strainer. Add champagne vinegar to taste for a little added brightness. Cool in fridge.
- Whip cream to stiff peaks. You do not need to sweeten cream, as I added some of the coulis to the cream to sweeten it and get a nice light color. I used about 3-4 Tablespoons of the coulis. Reserve in fridge.
- Chocolate Pasta
- Add flour, cocoa power, sugar and salt and mix thoroughly. Form a well in the center and add slightly beaten eggs.
- Mix around the egg to slowly incorporate the dry mixture, until it forms a shaggy dough.
- Knead dough for 5 - 10 minutes, until it bounces back when depressed. If it is very sticky add a little more flour, and knead some more. Then let it rest for about 1 hour in the fridge.
- Roll out dough on pasta machine from the thickest to thinnest setting. I stopped at 6 of 10, as the dough is a little trickier the thinner you go.
- Rest on flour board or kitchen towel to dry slight.
- Cut to preferred shape, I did my like pappardelle and small squares as well.
- Cook in rapidly boiling water for 2-5 minutes (depends on thickness and extent you let them dry). Then place in ice water.
- Dry pasta and plate. Enjoy!

31. Cockney Champagne Cocktail

Serving: Serves 1 | Prep: | Cook: |Ready in:

Ingredients

- 3/4 ounce gin
- 3/4 ounce freshly squeezed lemon juice
- 1/2 ounce simple syrup (1:1 sugar to water)
- 3 ounces Champagne

Direction

- Shake first three ingredients with ice. Strain into coupe or Champagne glass, and top with Champagne.

32. Coconut Banana Pancakes With Bacon And Berries

Serving: Makes 2 - 3 servings (double recipe for 4-5 servings) | Prep: | Cook: |Ready in:

Ingredients

- for the pancakes
- 1 1/2   mashed overripe bananas
- 4   eggs
- 1 teaspoon vanilla extract
- 1/8 - 1/4 cups water or vanilla almond milk
- 1/3 cup coconut flour
- 1 teaspoon baking powder
- 1 teaspoon salt
- 1 tablespoon coconut oil (for cooking)
- for the toppings:
- 1 cup mixed berries (fresh or frozen)
- 1 tablespoon honey
- 1 tablespoon lemon juice
- 1 tablespoon champagne vinegar
- 4   slices bacon

Direction

- Preheat oven to 400 degrees. Place bacon on a foil lined baking sheet and pop into the oven for about 15 minutes, until crisp. Remove from oven and place on a paper towel. Set aside until pancakes are ready.
- As bacon cooks make the berries and pancake batter. For the berries, place berries, honey, lemon juice and champagne vinegar in a small sauce pan over low heat. Let slowly cook down until everything else is ready. It will get runny and soft, like a sauce.
- Now for the pancakes. Make the batter. In 1 medium bowl whisk together eggs, mashed bananas, vanilla and water or almond milk. In a separate medium bowl combine coconut flour, baking powder and salt. Slowly add the wet ingredients to the dry ingredients and mix only to combine. Don't over mix.
- Heat a griddle or pan over medium to medium low heat and add coconut oil. Add pancake batter using a 1/4 cup. Cook for 3 minutes on one side, flip and cook for another 3 on the other. Watch to make sure they don't burn! Work in batches if necessary.
- Serve pancakes with berry sauce and crumbled bacon. Enjoy this gluten free, refined sugar free breakfast or brunch one of these weekends.

33. Composed Salad Of Smoked Salmon, Cucumber, Mâche, Egg, And Asparagus

Serving: Serves 4 | Prep: | Cook: |Ready in:

Ingredients

- For the vinaigrette:
- 3 tablespoons wal
- 2 tablespoons champagne vinegar
- 1 tablespoon chopped fresh dill
- 1/2 teaspoon kosher salt
- Freshly-ground black pepper
- For the salad:
- 1   package (4 ounces) mâche
- 12   spears of pickled asparagus
- 4   soft-boiled eggs, halved

- 8 ounces smoked salmon, sliced
- medium cucumber, thinly sliced
- 1 lemon, quartered

Direction

- To make the dressing, whisk walnut oil, champagne vinegar, dill, salt, and a few grinds of black pepper together in a small bowl until emulsified. Toss mâche with the dressing until coated.
- Distribute mâche between four salad plates or shallow bowls, then arrange three asparagus spears, one egg, two ounces of salmon, a quarter of the cucumber slices, and a lemon wedge on each plate. Serve immediately.

34. Crabe Beninoise, Avocado And Mango Salad

Serving: Serves 2-4 | Prep: | Cook: | Ready in:

Ingredients

- 1 champagne mango
- 1 hass avocado
- 1 scallion, chopped
- zest and fresh juice of 1 Lime
- salt and pepper to taste
- 1/2 cup mayonnaise
- 1 garlic clove, minced
- 1/2 teaspoon scotch bonnet, minced
- 6 ounces jumbo lump crabmeat
- 1 tablespoon chopped fresh cilantro
- 1 plum tomato, diced

Direction

- Dice champagne mango or regular mango and set aside in a medium-sized bowl. (Champagne mangos are less fibrous and have a thin pit.)
- Split the avocado in half and remove the pit. Dice the flesh and drop into a medium-sized

bowl. Add the zest and juice of lime and salt and pepper. Lightly toss.
- Combine crabmeat, chopped scallions, chopped cilantro, diced tomatoes, minced scotch bonnet, mayonnaise and salt and pepper to taste. Lightly toss.
- Use the crabmeat mixture to fill the bottom layer of a clear container. Repeat with the avocado mixture and then the diced mango. You can eat immediately, but it's best refrigerated for at least an hour.

35. Cranberry Apple Sparkling Punch

Serving: Serves 15-20 people | Prep: | Cook: | Ready in:

Ingredients

- 1 bottle dry prosecco or champagne
- 1 bottle 25. 4 oz. of sparkling apple juice (I like Knudson's)
- 1 bottle 25.4 oz. of sparkling cranberry juice
- 1/2 to 3/4 cups fresh lime juice
- 6-9 lady apples - as small as you can find

Direction

- The night before or several hours prior to assembling the punch, place lady apples in a few round containers, or in a Bundt pan and fill with water. Freeze.
- Pour cold prosecco or champagne and both bottles of sparkling juices in a large bowl. Stir well, and then add lime juice gradually according to your taste preference.
- Run warm water over the frozen containers to loosen the ice floes. Place in the bowl to keep punch cold.
- Serve with a small dollop of sorbet in each glass if you desire.

36. Crimson Bulleit Punch

Serving: Serves 1 to 100 | Prep: 0hours10mins | Cook: 0hours0mins | Ready in:

Ingredients

- 2   parts Bulleit bourbon
- 2   parts cranberry pomegranate juice
- 1/2   part Domaine de Canton ginger liquer
- 2   parts Champagne
- Lime slices
- Ice ring (if making for a punch bowl), or shaken with ice for individual servings

Direction

- Combine all ingredients in a punch bowl, adding the Champagne just before party time to better maintain its sparkle. Ladle chilled punch into glasses, garnish with a slice of lime and start singing with Burl.

37. Easy Lime Chickpea Salad

Serving: Serves 2 | Prep: | Cook: | Ready in:

Ingredients

- 31 ounces Chickpeas
- 1/3 cup Chopped Cilantro
- 2   Medium Tomatoes (Diced)
- 1/8 cup Champagne Vinegar
- 1   Lime (Juiced)
- Salt & Pepper to Taste
- 2 tablespoons Extra Virgin Olive Oil

Direction

- For this easy and quick salad, simply combine your chickpeas, cilantro and tomatoes in a bowl and mix.
- In a separate bowl, combine the lime juice, salt, pepper, champagne vinegar and olive oil and stir.

- Now pour your dressing over the chickpea, tomato and cilantro to finish off your salad.
- Enjoy!

38. Elk Milanesa With Lemon Caper Bechamel

Serving: Serves 2 | Prep: | Cook: | Ready in:

Ingredients

- Lemon Caper Bechamel
- 2 tablespoons unsalted butter
- 2 tablespoons flour
- 1   clove garlic - minced
- 1/2 cup buttermilk
- 1/2 cup champagne (you can use white wine too I jusy happened to have champagne open and ready)
- 1 teaspoon fresh thyme
- 2 tablespoons capers
- 1/4 cup lemon stilton
- a pinch each salt and pepper
- 1 tablespoon parmesan (I used reggiano)
- juice from a wedge of lemon
- Elk Milanesa
- 6   thin slices of elk backstrap
- 1   cup flour seasoned with salt and pepper
- 1 cup seasoned breadcrumbs
- 2   eggs
- juice from one lemon wedge
- 2 tablespoons butter
- 2 tablespoons olive oil

Direction

- Lemon Caper Béchamel
- Whisk the flour, garlic and butter together in a large saucepan over medium heat. After a few minutes whisk in the buttermilk and champagne, then the cheeses and the thyme. Squeeze the lemon and add the capers, stir and taste, adjust the salt and pepper

accordingly. Turn off the heat (if it gets too thick add a bit more milk)

- Elk Milanesa
- Put a cookie sheet lines with parchment in a 200 degree oven. Set up your breading station using 3 cake pans (or whatever your vessel of choice is) line them up - flour, egg whisked with lemon juice, then breadcrumb.
- Heat the butter and oil in a large skillet to med-high.
- Dredge your elk - flour then egg then breadcrumb then into the skillet, how many at a time depends on the size of the pan. Brown on one side, flip, brown on the other then into the oven until they are all cooked.
- Heat the béchamel back up (this is where you may need to add another dab of milk), then plate the milanesa, spoon béchamel over, and eat up

39. English 75

Serving: Makes 1 drink | Prep: | Cook: |Ready in:

Ingredients

- 2.5 ounces Hendrick's Gin
- 1.5 ounces freshly squeezed lemon or lime juice, or mixture
- Dash Rose water
- Champagne or prosecco
- Cucumber to garnish

Direction

- Shake gin, lemon juice, and rose water with ice until chilled.
- Strain into a chilled champagne flute and top with champagne or prosecco.
- Garnish with a thin wedge or slice of cucumber.

40. Eric Korsh's Farm Lettuces Salad With Dill Vinaigrette

Serving: Serves 4, with leftover vinaigrette | Prep: | Cook: |Ready in:

Ingredients

- Dill Vinaigrette
- 1   large egg
- 1 cup (25 grams) picked dill fronds (from about 1/2 bunch)
- 1 tablespoon plus 1 teaspoon (19 grams) Dijon mustard
- 3 1/2 tablespoons (50 grams) Champagne or white wine vinegar
- 1/4 cup neutral oil, like canola or grapeseed
- 1/4 cup olive oil
- Salt and freshly ground pepper, to taste
- Farm Lettuces Salad
- Lettuces of your choice (see note below) — enough for about 6 cups torn, washed and spun dry
- 1 cup crumbled fresh sheep's milk feta
- 2   scallions, thinly sliced
- 1/3 cup chives cut into 1-inch lengths

Direction

- Dill Vinaigrette
- Cook the egg in abundant boiling water for 7 minutes and 15 seconds, for barely set yolks and fully set whites. Rinse and peel in cold water to stop it from cooking further.
- Blend egg, dill, Dijon, and Champagne vinegar until smooth. Note: For a lighter-colored dressing with more bits of green in it, you can pulse in the herbs toward the end — this is especially good to do if substituting more strongly flavored herbs like chives for the dill.
- Mix canola oil and olive oil and slowly, with the blender running, drizzle oil mixture in until emulsified. Season with salt and pepper to taste.
- Any leftover dressing will keep in the fridge for 3 to 4 days, though the color and fresh herb flavor may fade slightly after a day.

- Farm Lettuces Salad
- In choosing the lettuces, the salad should be bright and fresh. The leaves should be light, but stout enough to hold the other ingredients. Use red oak, green oak, and/or butter lettuce.
- Just before serving, toss the lettuce with dressing to taste (it should be just enough to lightly coat the leaves), plus feta, scallions, and chives.

41. Evergreen

Serving: Serves 6 | Prep: | Cook: |Ready in:

Ingredients

- 3   oranges - juice
- 1/2   Pineapple
- 1/8 cup   Passion Fruit Syrup
- 8   fresh mint leaves
- Champagne to top

Direction

- Process half a peeled and cored pineapple. Divide the pulp in an ice cube tray and freeze for 1 hour – it should be slushy.
- With a hand held blender process the orange juice with the mint leaves. Sieve and process the juice with the Passion fruit syrup and the pineapple slush.
- Fill champagne flutes half with fruit mix and top with Champagne. Serve cold, decorated with a triangle of pineapple with the skin on.

42. Fall Beet Salad

Serving: Serves 4-6 | Prep: | Cook: |Ready in:

Ingredients

- 3   golden beets
- 3   red beets

- 1 cup   white wine
- 2   cloves garlic, smashed
- 1 bunch   swiss chard, stems removed, chopped
- 1   onion, julienne
- 1   shallot, minced
- 1   orange
- 2 tablespoons   honey
- 2 tablespoons   dried thyme
- 1 cup   champagne vinegar
- 3 cups   olive oil + a little more for roasting the beets
- 1/2 cup   pecan pieces, toasted
- 1/4 cup   fresh goat cheese, such as chevre

Direction

- Preheat oven to 400. Place beets in a roasting pan with wine, a little bit of water, and garlic cloves. Cover with aluminum foil and cook until tender, about one hour. Once beets are done cooking, remove from oven and peel skin off while still hot. Cut into small pieces and cool.
- Caramelize onions in a sauté pan over medium high heat. Cook until they are a golden brown color and add Swiss chard. Continue cooking for about 4 - 5 minutes more, or until greens have wilted. Season with a little salt and pepper. Cool
- To make the dressing, whisk orange juice, champagne vinegar, honey, thyme, and salt and pepper together. Slowly emulsify in the olive oil.
- Before serving, mix the beets, onions and chard mixture, dressing, pecans, and goat cheese together. Serve at room temperature.

43. Fig And Manchego Salad With Herbed Croutons

Serving: Serves 2 | Prep: | Cook: |Ready in:

Ingredients

- For the herbed croutons:

- two 1/2 inch-thick slices stale bread (I like sourdough)
- 1 large clove garlic, peeled
- 2 tablespoons extra-virgin olive oil
- 1 pinch sea salt
- 1 pinch ground black pepper
- 2 tablespoons minced mixed herbs (such as parsley, thyme, rosemary, chives, or tarragon)
- For the salad and vinaigrette:
- 1 clove garlic, peeled
- 1 pinch sea salt
- 1/2 teaspoon Dijon mustard
- 1/4 teaspoon honey
- 1 1/2 tablespoons champagne vinegar
- 3 tablespoons extra-virgin olive oil
- 1 tablespoon minced shallot
- 1 tablespoon minced mixed herbs
- 4 cups tender bitter greens, such as arugula, mustard greens, or mizuna
- 8 to 10 large figs, quartered
- 10 triangular slices Manchego cheese
- 2 triangular croutons

Direction

- For the herbed croutons:
- Rub each side of bread with the clove of garlic.
- Cut the bread into large triangles or cubes.
- Heat a heavy-bottomed skillet over medium heat. Add the olive oil. When the oil is warm, add the bread pieces. Add a sprinkle of sea salt and cook each side for 3 to 4 minutes, or until a deep golden brown. Toss with ground black pepper and herbs.
- For the salad and vinaigrette:
- Use a mortar and pestle to smash garlic and sea salt into a paste.
- Whisk the garlic mixture into the mustard, honey, and champagne vinegar, and then whisk in the olive oil. When mixture is emulsified, stir in shallots and herbs.
- In a large bowl, drizzle half the dressing over the greens and toss. Tuck figs and Manchego throughout. Toss gently, add a drizzle of dressing, and adjust seasoning. Plate each salad with two warm croutons.

44. First Kiss On A Ferris Wheel

Serving: Makes one drink | Prep: | Cook: | Ready in:

Ingredients

- 2 ounces Brugal Añejo Rum
- 3/4 ounce Lemon
- 1.5 ounces Butter Agave Syrup
- 4 Green Apple Slices
- 2 tablespoons White Sugar
- 1.25 tablespoons Ground Cinnamon
- 1.5 ounces Cava/ Champagne

Direction

- In a shaker tin, muddle the sectioned Apple Slices, Butter Agave Syrup, Rum, and lemon.
- Add Ice to the shaker tin, cap, and shake vigorously.
- Mix the sugar and cinnamon together on a small plate suitable for rimming a glass.
- Rim a coup glass with the cinnamon sugar mixture.
- Double Strain the drink in to the coup glass
- Top the drink with the Cava/ Champagne.

45. Fleur De Lys

Serving: Serves 1 | Prep: | Cook: | Ready in:

Ingredients

- 8 ounces fresh squeezed orange juice, chilled
- 1/2 tablespoon Pernod
- 2 tablespoons Cointreau
- sparkling mineral water (I like Gerolsteiner - tiny bubbles) or Champagne, chilled
- ice (optional)

Direction

- In a 10-ounce jar with a screw-on lid, or a cocktail shaker, combine orange juice and liqueurs. Shake well.
- If using ice cubes, place several in a glass of your choice.
- Pour orange juice mixture into glass. Top off with 1 or 2 glugs of chilled sparkling water or Champagne.
- Stir once and enjoy!

46. Flirtini

Serving: Serves one delicious pitcher | Prep: | Cook: | Ready in:

Ingredients

- 2 cups champagne
- 2 cups raspberry vodka
- 2 cups pineapple juice
- 2 cups orange juice (pulp free)

Direction

- Mix equal parts champagne, vodka (raspberry vodka, if you're feeling fancy) orange juice, pineapple juice. Chill and imbibe.

47. Frosted Ginger Peach Bellini

Serving: Serves 4 | Prep: | Cook: | Ready in:

Ingredients

- 5 ripe peaches
- 8 tablespoons sugar
- 1 bottle champagne or other sparkling wine
- 8 ounces ginger ale
- 2 cups ice

Direction

- Blanch peaches by immersing into boiling water for 30 seconds. Immediately remove peaches and place in a bowl of ice water to cool. As soon as they are cool enough to handle, peel the peaches.
- Slice peeled peaches into a blender or food processor. Add sugar and ice. Blend until smooth. If necessary, add a little water to help it blend. You may also add more sugar if the peaches are especially tart.
- Divide the peach mixture among four wine glasses. Pour 2 ounces of ginger ale into each glass, then fill to the top with champagne.

48. Game Hens With Roasted Grape Mostarda

Serving: Makes 4 game hens and mostarda | Prep: | Cook: | Ready in:

Ingredients

- Mustard-Roasted Game Hens
- 4 game hens (1 3/4 to 2 pounds each)
- 4 minced garlic cloves
- 4 tablespoons honey
- 4 tablespoons whole grain mustard
- 4 tablespoons olive oil
- 2 tablespoons minced fresh rosemary
- Salt and pepper
- Roasted Grape Mostarda
- 3 cups black seedless grapes
- 1/2 cup chopped shallot
- 3 tablespoons olive oil
- 1/4 cup white wine
- 2 tablespoons sugar
- 1/4 cup Champagne vinegar
- 1 tablespoon mustard seeds
- 1 bay leaf
- 1 teaspoon dry mustard
- 2 teaspoons Dijon mustard
- 1/4 cup reserved pan juices from game hens
- 1 tablespoon chopped fresh rosemary

Direction

- Mustard-Roasted Game Hens
- Preheat the oven to 400° F. Liberally season the game hens (inside and out) with salt and pepper. Allow them to sit out for up to an hour to lose the chill of the fridge.
- Mix the garlic, honey, whole grain mustard, olive oil, and rosemary in a bowl. Rub the mixture all over the inside and outside of the hens.
- Place the hens on a roasting rack and cook for about 60 minutes (depending on the size of your bird), until an instant read thermometer in the leg/thigh registers 170 degrees (or the juices run clear). Watch your birds carefully after 40 minutes or so to ensure the skin isn't turning too dark. I covered my birds with foil for the last 15 minutes or so.
- Rest the birds under a foil tent for 10 minutes before serving.
- Roasted Grape Mostarda
- Preheat your oven to 400° F (this can be done alongside the game hens). On a sheet pan place the grapes, shallots, rosemary, and olive oil. Season lightly with salt. Roast for 15 minutes, until the grapes have softened and the shallots have browned.
- Deglaze the baking sheet with the white wine immediately, scraping up any bits of browned grape and shallot. Pour the mixture on the baking sheet into a saucepan.
- Add the sugar, Champagne vinegar, mustard seed, dry mustard, and bay leaf to the grapes in the saucepan. Over medium heat, cook the mixture down until the grapes are very soft and most of the liquid has evaporated.
- Off the heat, add the reserved pan juices and Dijon and remove the bay leaf. Serve warm or at room temperature alongside the game hens. Crusty bread is recommended.

49. Geranium Fizz

Serving: Serves 2 | Prep: | Cook: |Ready in:

Ingredients

- 4-5 large fresh geranium leaves, roughly chopped
- 1/2-1 tablespoons sugar
- juice of half a lemon
- 1 ounce Lillet
- 2 ounces Gin
- Champagne to finish
- Lemon peel and small geranium leaf to garnish

Direction

- In a cocktail shaker, muddle the geranium leaves, sugar and lemon juice. I use about a 1/2 tablespoon of sugar because I like a stronger drink, rather than a sweeter drink.
- Add the Lillet, Gin, a handful of ice and shake.
- Strain into two champagne flutes, leaving about an inch and a half of space.
- Add the champagne.
- Garnish with the lemon peel and small geranium leaves.
- Drink, being grateful for Oracles and Spring.

50. Giddo's Dream Waffles

Serving: Makes 8-10 waffles | Prep: | Cook: |Ready in:

Ingredients

- Giddo's Dream Waffles
- 2 cups all purpose flour
- 1 teaspoon salt
- 4 teaspoons baking powder
- 2 tablespoons white sugar
- 2 eggs
- 1 1/2 cups crème fraiche (see recipe below)
- 1/3 cup melted and slightly browned butter
- 1 teaspoon vanilla extract

- 2/3 cup champagne
- 1 tablespoon lemon zest
- delicious maple syrup to taste!
- Crème Fraiche Recipe
- 2 cups heavy cream
- 3 tablespoons cultured buttermilk

Direction

- Giddo's Dream Waffles
- In a large bowl, mix together all dry ingredients. Set aside and preheat waffle iron to desired temperature.
- In a separate bowl, beat the eggs. Stir in the crème fraiche, butter, and vanilla. Pour the wet mixture into the flour and combine. Stir in the Champagne and lemon zest. Feel free to add more Champagne if needed to make it the correct consistency (really thick and gooey).
- Ladle the batter into a preheated waffle iron. Cook until golden & crisp. Serve immediately.
- Crème Fraiche Recipe
- Pour both cream and buttermilk into jar. Mix together and leave in a warm spot (about 70-75 degrees F.) for 24 hours, or until thick. Refrigerate for 24 hours before using. Should last a week or two.

51. Grilled Watermelon And Jicama Salad

Serving: Serves 4-6 | Prep: | Cook: | Ready in:

Ingredients

- 1 ounce pancetta, thin sliced
- 1/2 medium, (seedless) watermelon (about 4 cups cubed)
- 1 jicama
- 5 ounces baby arugula
- 3 ounces crumbled feta
- 1 teaspoon kosher salt
- 1/4 teaspoon fresh ground black pepper
- 1 tablespoon balsamic vinegar
- 1/2 tablespoon champagne vinegar

- 1/4 cup pickled red onion

Direction

- Lay your slices of pancetta on a sheet pan. Place the pan in the cold oven and set the temperature to 400 F. Bake until golden brown and crispy, about 15 minutes depending on how thinly your pancetta has been sliced. Allow to cool and crumble. Set aside.
- Peel the jicama. Cut into 1/8" julienne (carefully cut into 1/8" slices, then place each 1/8 inch disk flat on the cutting board and cut across into 1/8" matchsticks). Set aside.
- If using a gas grill, allow to preheat on high. If using charcoal, get a bed of hot, mature coals going. Meanwhile, remove the green and white peel from the watermelon with a serrated knife, so that only the red flesh remains. You don't have to use a seedless watermelon but if you don't you'll be spitting out some seeds as you eat this salad. Cut your melon into ~1/2" slices, and put them straight onto the grill.
- Grill the melon for 3-5 minutes per side, enough to get a noticeably charred from the grating but still solid enough to be flipped easily. Once grilled on both sides, allow to cool enough to handle before sprinkling with 1/4 tsp of kosher salt and cutting into 1/2" cubes.
- In a large salad bowl, combine the watermelon, jicama, arugula, and feta. Sprinkle with the balsamic and champagne vinegars, and the remaining salt and freshly ground black pepper. Add the pickled red onions and toss everything to combine.
- Sprinkle over the crumbled pancetta, and serve.

52. Hen Liver Pâté

Serving: Serves 2-3 | Prep: | Cook: | Ready in:

Ingredients

- 10 cornish game hen livers, cleaned of any fat
- 1 tablespoon butter
- 1 tablespoon olive oil
- 3 sage leaves, diced
- 1 small garlic clove, diced
- 1/3 cup champagne
- 1/2 lemon zest

Direction

- Clean the livers of any fat, dry them, and season with salt and pepper.
- Add the butter, sage, garlic, and oil to a pan, turn it up to high heat, and then add the livers. Cover and cook for 2-3 minutes.
- Add the champagne and cook down for 5 more minutes, or until the champagne has cooked down and only about 1/3 of it is left.
- Put into a food processor, or if you don't have one (like me), chop up finely and use an immersion blender. Add the lemon zest and season again to taste.
- Let cool and put in the fridge. After about an hour… pâté! It makes enough spread for about 3 leftover dinner rolls, sliced up, and toasted.

53. Herbed Salmon With Creamy Champagne Mushroom Sauce

Serving: Serves 4 | Prep: | Cook: | Ready in:

Ingredients

- 4 salmon fillets, 1-inch thick, skin removed
- 4 tablespoons butter
- 1 tablespoon fresh thyme leaves
- 2 cups fresh sliced mushrooms
- 2 tablespoons fresh lemon juice
- 1/2 cup champagne (or white wine)
- 2 tablespoons flour
- 1 cup heavy cream
- Thyme sprigs for garnish

Direction

- Melt butter in large skillet over medium-high heat.
- Sauté fresh thyme leaves in butter 1 minute, or until fragrant.
- Add salmon fillets to skillet in single layer. Baste fillets thoroughly with butter.
- Add mushrooms to skillet.
- Pour lemon juice and champagne over all.
- Reduce heat to medium-low. Cover skillet and simmer 25 minutes, or until salmon flakes easily with fork.
- Transfer salmon to plate.
- Sprinkle flour over mushrooms and drippings in skillet. Increase heat to medium-high and cook, stirring, 1 minute.
- Whisk in cream and cook, stirring, 2 minutes more, or until sauce is thickened.
- Return salmon to skillet to heat through.
- To serve, place salmon on plates. Spoon sauce over top. Garnish with thyme sprigs.

54. Honey Tangerine Champagne Punch With Black Cherry Granita

Serving: Serves 10-12 | Prep: | Cook: | Ready in:

Ingredients

- The juice, simple syrup and granita
- 8-10 honey tangerines (should make approximately 3 cups of juice)
- 6 navel oranges (should make approximately 3 cups of juice)
- the zest of 2 tangerines or 1 navel orange
- 1/2 cup sugar (for simple syrup)
- 1/2 cup water (for simple syrup
- 1 quart black cherry juice no sugar added (I used R.W Knudson) (for granita)
- 2 tablespoons creme de Mure or cassis (for granita)
- 1/2 cup sugar (for granita)
- 1 teaspoon lemon zest (for granita)
- Putting it all together

- 6 cups tangerine/orange juice (48 oz)
- 1 1/2 - 2 bottles champagne (the amount of champagne depends on how boozy you want the punch)
- 1/4 cup tangerine simple syrup
- black cherry granita

Direction

- The juice, simple syrup and granita
- To make the simple syrup, in med saucepan add sugar, water and tangerine or orange zest. Bring to a boil, don't stir just swirl the pot to make sure no sugar crystals stick to the side of the pan. When all of the sugar is dissolved remove from heat, let come to room temperature pour through sieve into jar and refrigerate until ready to use.
- In same saucepan add black cherry juice, sugar and lemon zest bring to a boil, stir frequently and remove from heat when sugar is dissolved. Add the crème de mure or cassis. Bring to room temperature or to quicken the process put in ice bath to get it cold and pour into rectangular non-reactive pan. Place in freezer for approximately 1 1/2 hours, (you will see the edges starting to freeze) using a fork scrape and put back in freezer, repeat this process every hour until its frozen through and resembles shaved ice. Cover and keep frozen. It takes about 3-4 hours to make this.
- Juice your tangerines and oranges and refrigerate. All ingredients should be cold when you assemble the punch. Chill your champagne.
- Putting it all together
- Chill your punch bowl. Add juice and simple syrup and stir to combine. Add the champagne. Have your glasses or champagne flutes ready. To serve, scoop a heaping tablespoon of granita into glass, ladle punch over the granita and enjoy!
- Note: This can be made with seltzer or sparkling water instead of champagne for a booze free punch if you use sparkling water add 1/2 cup simple syrup.

55. Hot Potato Salad (with Chive, Curry Dressing)

Serving: Serves 8 | Prep: | Cook: |Ready in:

Ingredients

- 6 red russet potatoes
- 6 cloves of garlic, peeled
- 1 medium sized bulb of fennel, stem removed
- 1 fuji apple
- 1 leek, white part only
- 2 teaspoons olive oil
- 1/4 teaspoon champagne vinegar
- 2 tablespoons chives, chopped
- 1/4 teaspoon mustard powder
- 1/4 teaspoon curry powder
- 1/4 teaspoon white pepper
- 1/4 cup quinoa, rinsed

Direction

- Begin boiling a large pot over water over medium-high heat and set oven to 420 degrees.
- Wash the potatoes and place them in the pot of water (once it has a rolling boil) for ten minutes (or until softened, not mushy). Remove the potatoes and rinse under cool water. Let them sit while you prep the rest of the ingredients.
- Cut garlic into thin slices along the width of the clove. Cut the white part of the leek (save the greens for another dish) into thin slices as well. Dice apple and fennel into equal sized cubes.
- Once the potatoes have cooled to the touch, dice them into larger cubes (about a 1/2 inch long).
- In a high-sided oven pan, mix the fennel, garlic, and potatoes with a little bit of olive oil. Spread on the pan so that the potatoes all have contact with the metal sheet. Bake for 40 minutes, until crisp and golden brown. But

check every ten minutes to stir the ingredients so that none of them stick to the sheet or burn.

- While the potatoes are baking, place quinoa and 1 cup of water in a small pot. Bring to a boil and then reduce to a low simmer. Cook quinoa until all the water has been absorbed.
- While quinoa is cooking, mix your dressing: olive oil, mustard, white pepper, curry, and champagne vinegar.
- When the potatoes are nice and crisp, mix with apples, dressing, quinoa, and freshly cut chives. Serve immediately while it is warm!

56. Isabelle's Cognac Punch

Serving: Makes a sizable punchbowl | Prep: | Cook: | Ready in:

Ingredients

- 4   lemons
- 3 tablespoons Cognac
- 1 cup plus 5 tablespoons granulated sugar
- 3   bottles dry white wine
- 1   bottle Champagne, or other dry sparkling wine

Direction

- The day or night before the party, cut 3 of the lemons into slices. In a mortar and pestle, rough them up with the Cognac and the sugar. Cover with plastic, and refrigerate, at least 4 hours.
- In a punch bowl, pour in the sugar/Cognac mixture; discard the lemon slices. Pour in all the white wine, and stir to incorporate. Slice the remaining lemon, and let them float at the top of the punch bowl.
- Right before serving, pour in the Champagne. Give it a quick stir to mix, and voila!

57. Italian Sausage Pasta Dijonaise

Serving: Serves 4 | Prep: | Cook: | Ready in:

Ingredients

- 2   italian sausages
- 1   red bell pepper sliced
- 1 pint mushrooms
- 1 pound rigatoni or penne
- 1/2 cup champagne
- 1/4 to 1/2 cups white wine
- 2-3 tsp   dijon mustard
- 2-3 tbsp   marscapone
- 1/3 cup Chopped fresh parsley

Direction

- Put water on for pasta. In skillet, cook sausage till just tender remove to bowl. Add red pepper and remove to bowl. Add mushroom sauté till tender remove to bowl. Cook pasta till al dente. Add little water to Dijon to liquefy in pan. Over slow heat add Mascarpone. Add white wine 1/4 to 1/2 cup. Over low heat stir. Taste add 1/2 cup champagne. Cook down by half.
- Turn heat off. Chop 1/2 cup fresh flat leaf parsley set aside. Drain pasta leaving 1/2 cup pasta water for Dijon sauce Add el dente pasta to Dijon Fold in sausage, peppers and mushroom to pasta mixture. Add parsley. Fold in. Enjoy!

58. Jelly Bean Mimosas

Serving: Makes enough for about 6 cocktails | Prep: | Cook: | Ready in:

Ingredients

- 1 cup vodka
- 2 to 3 tablespoons jelly beans of a single flavor of your choice
- 1   lemon

- dry Champagne or other sparkling wine like cava or prosecco

Direction

- Combine the vodka and jelly beans in a jar and seal. Allow to sit for about 2 hours, shaking occasionally. Take a little taste to make sure jelly bean flavor and sweetness has infused into the vodka, then strain it through a fine strainer.
- To make a drink, add 1 ounce of the jelly bean-infused vodka (I call it jelly bean liqueur because it sounds fancy) and a little squeeze of lemon juice to a Champagne flute or coupe and top with chilled Champagne.

59. Kale Salad With A Garlic Caper Vinaigrette

Serving: Makes salad or a side for (1-2) | Prep: | Cook: |Ready in:

Ingredients

- 4 cups Kale - (1) big bunch
- 2   Garlic Cloves
- 2 tablespoons Capers - salted, not brined
- 6   Sun Dried Tomatoes - Halves
- 1 tablespoon Dijon Mustard
- 1 tablespoon Champagne Vinegar
- 2 tablespoons Pecorino - grated
- 1/4 cup Olive Oil - extra virgin

Direction

- Prep the Kale - cut across the bunch in 1" - 2" sections. No stems please. Wash and spin to dry. Set aside. Toast pine nuts in a sauté pan or in the oven till a pale shade of brown. Set aside.
- Mince the garlic. Chop the capers. Heat 1T olive oil (medium heat) in a sauté pan and briefly sauté the garlic for about a minute till translucent. Add chopped capers and

incorporate and heat through. Take off heat and scrape into a mixing bowl. Add the Dijon, champagne vinegar and a squeeze of 1/2 a lemon. Whisk and set aside.

- Set up a steamer and get the heat on. When the water is hot take away the steamer and dunk the sun dried tomatoes in the water for 3-4 minutes to let them re-hydrate. Pull from the water, cool slightly and then slice into strips. Set aside.
- Finish the vinaigrette. Whisk in 1/4 C of evoo into the mixing bowl. The Dijon should emulsify this vinaigrette nicely. Taste and adjust with lemon, salt, freshly ground pepper. This is too much vinaigrette for this dish yet the excess could find its way onto some seared halibut, salmon, arugula - your call.
- With the steamer on high add the kale and steam for (3-4) minutes. This happens quickly and - of course - you want the toothsome quality of kale so keep an eye on it!
- Remove Kale from the steamer and dump into a large plate and spread out. Chill in the fridge. Conversely I could say shock in a cold water bath yet then you are adding a water element back to the tortured kale - there is only so much time in the day to deal with drying again.
- Room temp or chilled kale gets tossed with the tasty vinaigrette (to your taste), a good portion of pine nuts and the sun dried tomatoes. Top with a sprinkling of pecorino. I feel pecorino stands up to robust kale.
- I can't tell you how to compose this salad to your taste however I love the play of leafy kale to a gutsy vinaigrette to oddly creamy pine nuts. Oh - and the forgotten sun dried tomato...
- Enjoy!

60. Kir Royales

Serving: Serves 6 | Prep: | Cook: |Ready in:

Ingredients

- 3 tablespoons creme de cassis
- 750 milliliters good Champagne
- 6 sprigs (twists) lemon

Direction

- Fill the bottom of 6 Champagne glasses with 1/2 tablespoon crème de cassis. Pop open a bottle of champagne and divide among the glasses. The color of the drink will be a sunset pink. Garnish with lemon twists.

61. Kiss The Ring, A Riff On The French 75

Serving: Makes 1 cocktail | Prep: 0hours5mins | Cook: 0hours0mins | Ready in:

Ingredients

- 1 ounce gin
- 3/4 ounce Cointreau
- 3/4 ounce fresh-squeezed blood orange juice
- Prosecco, for topping
- 1 strip blood orange zest (garnish)

Direction

- Shake the gin, Cointreau, and blood orange juice in shaker filled with ice. Double strain into a flute or coupe and top with Prosecco. Garnish with a strip of blood orange zest (squeeze the zest over the cocktail to release the essential oils, then run the zest strip around rim of glass before plopping in the cocktail).

62. Kumquat Marmalade With Champagne And Figs

Serving: Makes approx. 1 pint | Prep: | Cook: | Ready in:

Ingredients

- 3 1/2 cups champagne
- 1/2 cup honey
- 2 sticks cinnamon
- 4 cardamom pods
- approx. 40 kumquats
- approx. 20 dried figs
- 1/2 cup raisins
- 1 teaspoon vanilla extract
- 1 tablespoon rose water-optional

Direction

- In a medium-sized pot on the stove, bring the champagne and honey to a boil. Reduce the heat to a simmer, and add the cinnamon sticks and the cardamom pods.
- Roughly chop the kumquats and remove as many seeds as possible. You'll be able to remove more later, but if a few remain, they won't harm you. Add to the champagne and honey. Add the dried fruits and allow to simmer for about 30 minutes, or until the kumquats and dried fruits are very tender and the mixture is fairly thick. Remove and discard any visible remaining kumquat seeds, as well as the cinnamon sticks.
- Turn off the heat and allow the marmalade to cool. Process in a high speed blender or food processor to break up any large chucks of fruit and to pulverize the cardamom. Return to the pot and add the vanilla and optional rose water. Mix well, and then spoon into glass jar(s). Store in the refrigerator; it will keep for a week or two.

63. LEMONY PINK CHAMPAGNE MINI CAKES

Serving: Makes 8 large cupcakes | Prep: | Cook: | Ready in:

Ingredients

- For the cake...
- 120 grams butter, softened
- 200 grams caster sugar
- 1 teaspoon vanilla extract
- 50 grams ground almonds
- 1 cup pink champagne or prosecco
- zest of one lemon
- For the icing
- 150 grams butter, softened
- 2 cups icing sugar, sifted
- 2 tablespoons pink champagne or prosecco (at room temp)
- finely grated zest of half a lemon
- OPTIONAL: Spray roses (to decorate)

Direction

- Preheat oven to 180C fan bake. Place greaseproof liners into 8 holes of a large muffin tray. In the bowl of an electric mixer, beat butter and sugar until pale, light and fluffy. Add vanilla and then egg whites, one at a time, beating well after each addition. Refrigerate yolks to use another time.
- Combine flour, ground almonds and baking powder. Add half into the mixture, stir until just mixed, then repeat with second half. Next, add the pink champagne/Prosecco and lemon zest. Stop your electric mixer once all the ingredients are combined, be careful not to over mix.
- Divide the batter evenly between the muffin holes. Bake for approximately 30 minutes or until golden in color and springy to the touch. Allow the cakes to cool for around 10 minutes before turning onto a cooling rack.
- Meanwhile, make the icing: in the bowl of an electric mixer beat butter and icing sugar until smooth, pale and fluffy. Gradually add in the pink champagne/Prosecco, vanilla and lemon zest and continue beating until smooth and creamy.
- Once the mini cakes are cool, use a piping bag to pipe some icing onto each one in a swirling motion. Decorate with fresh spray roses and serve with a glass of pink champagne, of course!

- Store mini cakes in an airtight container in the fridge for up to 3 days.

64. Lagosta Suada Portugal Lobster In Tomato And Wine Sauce

Serving: Serves 4 | Prep: | Cook: | Ready in:

Ingredients

- 2 pounds lobster big, live
- 3 onions, medium, yellow
- 5 cups tomatoes very ripe, peeled and chopped
- 2 garlic cloves
- 2/3 cup Extra Virgin Olive Oil
- 1 cup Champagne or Sauternes white wine
- 6 tablespoons Port Wine
- 1 bay leaf
- 2 teaspoons Paprika
- 8 black peppercorns whole
- salt
- 1/4 cup parsley leaves chopped finely

Direction

- Thinly slice the onions, garlic (remove green part from inside). Chop finely the parsley for the garnish.
- Blanch the tomatoes, skin them and cut them in pieces and put them in a colander to drain any the excess water.
- Prepare the lobster: To kill the lobster as quickly and painlessly as possible, lay it flat on a chopping board, tailing facing away from you. Hold the lobster with a cloth so you don't prick yourself and insert the point of a heavy sharp knife into the head, aiming for the point one inch above the middle of the eyes. Press in one go until it goes all the way through the lobster's head to the cutting board, then bring the blade down between the eyes to finish the cut of the head. (If you can't do this, bring a pot of water to a boil and insert the lobster,

head first and let cook for 2 minutes maximum to kill the lobster).

- Cut the head in half, and discard the sac behind the eyes. Cut the body lengthwise, remove the black vein, then rotate the lobster horizontally and cut through the rings. Set aside in a bowl until you have all the lobsters cut.
- In a large wide pot with a tight fitting lid over medium high heat, add the Olive Oil, the onion and the black peppercorns and let sweat. Add the garlic, the bay leaf, the lobster pieces including head and claws and any juices that have come out of the lobster. Sauté until the shells change color (from dark red brown to bright red).
- Add the Champagne or white wine, let the alcohol evaporate completely, add the tomatoes, the paprika and a little salt and cover with a tight fitting lid. Lower the heat and let simmer for 20 minutes, shaking the pan from time to time.
- Uncover, add the Port Wine, let simmer for a further 15 minutes uncovered. Season with more salt if necessary. (Don't overcook the lobster as it will become rubbery). Discard the bay leaf.
- Serve hot, sprinkled with parsley. Serve with white Basmati rice or on top of slices of Italian bread. It is also brilliant if you shell the lobster and serve it with the sauce with linguini!
- Pair with the same wine you used for cooking, either Champagne or a California Sauternes wine.

65. Lemon Tri Color Quinoa Tabbouleh

Serving: Serves 6-8 | Prep: | Cook: | Ready in:

Ingredients

- 1 cup tri-color quinoa
- 1 1/2 cups water

- 1/2 bunch watercress or other green (like parsley or cilantro)
- 1/2 bunch mint
- 6-8 mini red, yellow orange peppers, diced (or use 1/2 each of red, yellow, orange bell peppers)
- 1/2 cup heirloom cherry tomatoes, diced
- 1 cucumber, seeded and diced
- 1/4 cup flavored olive oil (I used a harissa flavored one)
- 1/4 cup neutral oil
- 1/4 cup orange champagne vinegar (I used the one from trader joes)
- 1 lemon, juiced
- kosher salt and fresh cracked pepper, to taste.

Direction

- Boil quinoa in 1 1/2 c. of salted water...turn down immediately to a low simmer, cover and cook 10 minutes. Take off heat, let stand 5 minutes. You can then chill grains overnight. If prepping for the next day, wait to add dressing before using, or bring an additional amount to add.
- Add diced veggies and herbs. Original tabbouleh calls for flat leafed parsley but I like the peppery flavor of watercress and the zing of mint.
- Mix together oils and vinegar with lemon juice and salt and pepper with a whisk. If you want a bit of sweetness, but don't have an orange Muscat champagne vinegar, add 1 T. orange marmalade or honey and 1 T. OJ to 1/4 c. vinegar.
- Serve with baked pita chips or torn pieces of warm pita bread.
- This salad is great for vegans, vegetarians and those with gluten sensitivities...if you want to make it more of a main dish salad, add some roasted chicken or fish (or for those vegan/vegetarian friends, grilled tempeh)

66. Limoncello Rosemary Spritzer

Serving: Serves 2 | Prep: | Cook: |Ready in:

Ingredients

- For the limoncello
- 20 lemons, washed and dried
- 2 liters 100 proof bottles of vodka
- 4 cups superfine granulated sugar
- 5 cups water
- For the spritzer
- Seltzer or Champagne
- Fresh rosemary sprigs
- 2 ounces Limoncello

Direction

- Wash the lemons and dry them well. Zest the lemons with a fine micro plane. Get as much of the yellow as you can -- but avoid zesting the white pith. Put the zest in a 1 gallon glass jar that you've washed in hot soapy water and dried before using. Add one bottle of the vodka. Be sure to save the empty bottle. Cover the mouth of the jar with plastic wrap and then screw on the lid. Give the jar a shake and let it sit in a cool, dark place for a minimum of 2 weeks. I let it sit for at least a month or even two months if I want a really intense flavor.
- Combine the sugar and water in a saucepan and cook until the sugar has dissolved for 5 to 7 minutes to make a slightly thick simple syrup. Cool the syrup completely before you add it to the lemon/vodka mixture in the glass jar. Then add the second bottle of vodka to the jar filled with lemon pith and vodka, and let this sugar/lemon/vodka mixture rest for another 2 weeks (minimum) to 1-2 months. Hold on to the second empty bottle, too.
- When you're ready to use the Limon cello, line a mesh strainer with cheesecloth and dump the lemon/sugar/vodka mixture into the lined strainer that's been placed over a large bowl. Squeeze out as much liquid as you can and discard the pulp. Pour the remaining liquid into the two saved vodka bottles and store the Limon cello in the freezer until you're ready to use it. (You should taste it before pouring into the reserved vodka bottles. Here's your chance to adjust the sweetness if you think you need to add more simple syrup.)
- To make the spritzer pour 1 ounce of chilled Limon cello in each Champagne flute. Add enough cold seltzer or chilled Champagne to make the drink as concentrated as you'd like. Garnish with a sprig of fresh rosemary. (You can also finely chop rosemary and mix it with the Limon cello before you add the seltzer or Champagne to give a more pronounced flavor.)

67. Lychee And Ginger Ice Cream Sauce And Bellini.

Serving: Serves makes 3 cups sauce and 6 bellini. | Prep: | Cook: |Ready in:

Ingredients

- Lychee and Ginger Ice Cream Sauce.
- • ¼ cup sugar
- • 1 tablespoon cornstarch
- • 1 can (15oz) lychees
- • 1 tablespoon butter
- • 1 tablespoon candied ginger, minced
- • 2 tablespoons lime juice
- Bellini.
- • ½ inch slice fresh ginger, with skin
- • ½ cup granulated sugar
- • 1 cup cold water
- • 1 can (15oz) lychees drained and then semi-frozen
- • 3-4 tablespoons lime juice
- • 1 bottle Champagne or Sparkling Wine chilled

Direction

- To make Lychee Sauce: Mix together sugar and cornstarch in a sauce pan. Drain syrup from lychees (about 1 cup) and blend into cornstarch mixture. Add butter and ginger and cook, stirring, until sauce bubbles and thickens (about 2 minutes). Remove from heat and stir in lychees and lime juice. Serve warm or room temperature spooned over ice cream.

- For the Bellini: Begin by making the ginger simple syrup. Peel and grate the ginger. Add it together with the sugar and cold water to a saucepan. Bring it to a boil and stir until the sugar dissolves. Cover and let steep for 15 minutes. Strain, discard ginger pieces and set simple syrup aside.
- In a blender add lychees and blend until completely pureed. Add ginger simple syrup, lime juice and the syrup from drained lychees, blend and then place into the refrigerator to cool.
- For serving: Pour puree to a cocktail shaker, top off with Champagne and shake vigorously to combine. Pour into Champagne or any tall glasses and repeat process as needed.

68. Mamma's Strawberry Risotto

Serving: Serves 4 | Prep: | Cook: |Ready in:

Ingredients

- 2 cups Par-boiled Baldo Brown Rice for risotto (as indicated in the note above)
- 200 grams Fresh Organic Strawberries (about 12 small strawberries + a few more for garnish)
- 1 Shallot, finely diced
- 5-6 cups Vegetable Broth
- 1/2 tablespoon Extra Virgin Olive Oil
- Pinch Sea Salt
- 1/2 cup White Wine or Champagne (optional)
- dollop dashes Vegan Butter (optional)
- Drop Sugar Free Balsamic Vinegar Glaze (optional)

Direction

- Prepare homemade broth or heat store-bought broth (preferably low sodium and diluted in

water to lighten the flavor) in a pot and keep hot throughout the cooking process, as indicated in point 6 above.

- Heat oil in a wok or skillet over medium heat. Add finely diced shallots and a pinch of salt and sauté for 2-3 minutes.
- Add cooled, par-boiled rice to a very hot pan and dry toast the grains for 2-3 minutes until slightly translucent and hot to the touch (do not brown the rice)
- Add wine or champagne, if using, and let cook for 5 minutes to allow the alcohol to evaporate.
- Add sautéed onions to the toasted rice and mix to combine.
- Cover in broth (about 3-4 ladles), stir and let simmer on medium-low heat.
- Once broth has been partially absorbed, add another ladle of broth to just cover the rice, stir then let simmer. Repeat this step several times until rice is cooked, but still firm to the bite (al dente). The texture of the risotto should be creamy, not runny or clumpy.
- In the final step, you can add a dollop of vegan butter or Almond Butter Cream to the risotto (optional) and a drizzle of balsamic glaze (optional) and stir it throughout before plating and serving.
- Garnish with fresh strawberries and serve hot - buon appetito!

69. Megmosa

Serving: Serves 1 | Prep: | Cook: |Ready in:

Ingredients

- 2.5 ounces Champagne or Sparkling Wine
- 2.5 ounces Grapefruit Juice
- 3 pieces Raspberries

Direction

- Pour champagne (or sparkling wine) and grapefruit juice into flute glass.
- Garnish with raspberries.

- Serve chilled.

70. Mimosa Coffee Cake

Serving: Serves 8-10 | Prep: | Cook: |Ready in:

Ingredients

- Cake
- 1.5 cups all-purpose flour
- 1 teaspoon baking powder
- 1 teaspoon ground cinnamon
- 1/4 teaspoon salt
- 1/2 cup butter or dairy-free margarine
- 2/3 cup granulated sugar
- 3   eggs
- 2 tablespoons mayonnaise (light is fine)
- 1 teaspoon orange extract
- zest from 1 orange
- 2 tablespoons orange juice (about 1/2 orange)
- 6 tablespoons champagne
- Topping and Icing
- 4 tablespoons butter or dairy-free margarine, melted
- 1/2 cup all-purpose flour
- 3 tablespoons brown sugar
- 1/2 teaspoon ground cinnamon
- 1 cup powdered sugar
- 2 tablespoons champagne
- 1 teaspoon orange zest

Direction

- Preheat the oven to 350 degrees. Grease and flour a 9-inch springform pan.
- Prepare the topping: in a medium bowl, mix together the dry ingredients (1/2 cup flour, 3 tablespoons brown sugar, 1/2 teaspoon ground cinnamon). Pour in the 4 tablespoons of melted butter/margarine and mix with a fork until all the dry ingredients are coated and small clusters form. Set aside.
- Combine the dry ingredients for the cake: flour, baking, soda, cinnamon, and salt. Set aside.
- In the bowl of a mixer, cream together the butter and sugar until smooth. Add the eggs one at a time, mixing in between each one. Add the mayonnaise, orange extract, orange zest, and orange juice to the margarine/sugar/eggs mixture and stir until combined. Stir in the dry ingredients. Pour in the champagne and fold gently (by hand) until just combined.
- Transfer the batter into the prepared springform pan. Sprinkle the topping evenly over the batter. Bake for 30-35 minutes, or until an inserted toothpick comes out clean.
- Prepare the icing: mix together the powdered sugar and champagne until smooth. Stir in the orange zest. Drizzle over the cake, once the cake has cooled slightly.

71. More Bubbles No Troubles

Serving: Serves 1 | Prep: | Cook: |Ready in:

Ingredients

- 1 ounce gin
- 1/2 ounce lemon juice
- 1/2 ounce strawberry syrup (see syrup)
- 2-4 pieces mint leaves
- Champagne

Direction

- In a shaker tin, add gin, lemon juice, strawberry syrup and mint leaves.
- Fill the shaker halfway with ice and shake.
- After shaken, add about 1 1/2 - 2 oz. of champagne to your tin.
- Fine strain all ingredients into your Champagne flute.
- Garnish with a lemon twist and serve!

72. Mother's Ruin Punch

Serving: Serves 4 to 6 | Prep: | Cook: | Ready in:

Ingredients

- For the cinnamon orange tea-infused sweet vermouth:
- 3 tablespoons loose cinnamon-orange tea (they use Market Spice)
- one   750 milliliter bottle sweet vermouth (they use Martini)
- For the punch:
- 8   white sugar cubes
- 2 ounces club soda
- 4 ounces gin (they use Plymouth)
- 2 ounces tea-infused sweet vermouth
- 4 ounces grapefruit juice
- 2 ounces lemon juice
- 3 ounces dry Champagne
- Grapefruit wheels, for garnish

Direction

- Stir the bottle of vermouth and tea together, and let stand at room temperature for about an hour and a half, stirring occasionally. Strain through cheesecloth-lined sieve.
- In a pitcher or medium container, muddle the sugar cubes with the club soda until the sugar is broken up. Add everything else, save for the Champagne, and fill the container with ice. Stir until cold, then strain into a punch bowl over a large block of ice. (Alternatively, serve in individual glasses over ice.)
- Top with Champagne, and garnish with a grapefruit wheels.

73. Negroni Sbagliato Punch

*Serving: Serves 12 people twice | Prep: 0hours15mins |
Cook: 0hours5mins |Ready in:*

Ingredients

- For the ice molds:
- 2 oranges, sliced into thin rounds
- 1 1/2 cups fresh cranberries
- 10-15   small rosemary sprigs
- 9   whole star anise
- For the punch:
- 1-2 (750 ml) bottles Prosecco or other dry sparkling wine
- 1 (750 ml) bottle Campari
- 1 (750 ml) bottle sweet vermouth (I like Carpano Antica, but Martini Rosso will make your finished punch a more brilliant red color)
- 1   bottle seltzer (optional)

Direction

- For the ice molds:
- Divide the fruit and spices among 3 molds, bowls, cake pans, or Bundt pans. Fill with water (use distilled for slightly clearer ice), cover with plastic wrap or a plate, and freeze until solid. When you're ready to use one, loosen with a little bit of hot water and then add to your punch-bowl, pretty side up (whatever that means to you!).
- For the punch:
- Combine all ingredients in your punch bowl. For a lighter punch, top off with more Prosecco or with seltzer. If you plan on refreshing your punch through the night, double the recipe and refresh with equal parts all ingredients in any amount you please throughout the night (I do half-bottles at a time).

74. New Year's Champagne And Scampi Risotto

Serving: Serves 6 | Prep: | Cook: |Ready in:

Ingredients

- 2 cups Carnaroli fine rice (not parboiled)
- 1 cup very light vegetable broth (you might not need it all)

- 1 bottle of good Champagne (750ml)
- 3 shallots very finely chopped
- 4 tablespoons butter
- 1/4 cup cream
- 18 very fresh Scampi, no skin or head and deveined
- 1 tablespoon fresh parsley finely chopped
- black pepper
- salt

Direction

- Clean the Scampi removing head, skin and deveining them. Set aside.
- Peel and chop very finely the shallots.
- Put the Champagne in a pan and warm it up.
- Put the vegetable broth in a pan and keep it over low heat so it is always hot.
- In a pan melt 2 tablespoons of butter over medium heat, add the other shallot and allow to cook for 5 minutes until translucent. Add the rice and fry until well coated in oil and lightly translucent.
- Add the 750ml of warm Champagne all at once, stir and allow the risotto to simmer gently (uncovered).
- When the rice is almost dry, add enough broth to continue cooking until al dente (more or less 15 minutes).
- Meanwhile, melt the other 2 tablespoons of butter and lightly sauté the Scampi. Season with salt and pepper. Chop in 2 or 3 pieces 6 scampi and keep the others for garnish. Keep warm covering with an aluminum foil.
- Warm up the cream but don't let it boil.
- After 15 minutes, remove from the heat. Check the seasoning and add some freshly grated black pepper, the hot cream and stir vigorously with a wooden spoon to cream the risotto. Check the seasoning. Add half the scampi and any juices from the pan and mix gently. Cover and let rest for 3 minutes before serving.
- Plate the risotto, garnish with 2 Scampi per plate, sprinkle with some chopped parsley and freshly ground black pepper.

- In Italy we don't serve Parmesan dish with any fish or shellfish so this risotto doesn't call for any cheese but feel free to add if you like it.

75. Nineteenth Century: Roman Punch

Serving: Makes 6 to 8 drinks | Prep: | Cook: | Ready in:

Ingredients

- 2 cups lemonade
- Juice of 2 oranges
- 8 ounces Champagne
- 8 ounces rum
- 2 large egg whites
- A few drops lemon juice
- 3 cups confectioners' sugar

Direction

- Stir together the lemonade, orange juice, Champagne, and rum in a punch bowl. Chill.
- When ready to serve, make the meringue: whip the egg whites and lemon juice in a medium bowl until they hold soft peaks, then gradually beat in the confectioners' sugar. Pile into a serving bowl.
- Fill punch cups with ice, ladle over the punch, and top each with a dollop of meringue. Serve with cocktail stirrers.

76. One Cup Punch

Serving: Serves 12 | Prep: | Cook: | Ready in:

Ingredients

- 1.5 liters cheap champagne (i.e. Andre's) - may be flavored if you like
- 12 ounces grenadine (i.e. Rose's)
- 375 milliliters brandy (i.e. E&J)

Direction

- Pour champagne slowly into a large punch bowl.
- Add brandy.
- Add grenadine to taste (if you purchased flavored champagne, you might not need as much grenadine).
- Add ice cubes if desired.
- Stir. Drink slowly.

---

77. Orzo Salad With Scallions, Hazelnuts, And Golden Raisins

Serving: Makes 1 quart | Prep: | Cook: |Ready in:

Ingredients

- 1/2 cup hazelnuts
- 1/2 cup red wine vinegar
- 1/2 cup golden raisins
- 1 cup orzo
- 1 lime, juiced
- 2 tablespoons rice wine vinegar
- 2 tablespoons champagne vinegar
- Kosher salt
- 1/4 cup sesame oil
- 2 tablespoons good olive oil, plus more for coating the orzo
- 6 scallions
- Small handful of chives
- 1/4 teaspoon red pepper flakes
- 2 ounces fresh goat cheese
- 1/4 teaspoon flaky sea salt

Direction

- Heat the oven to 350° F. Scatter the hazelnuts across a baking sheet, then put in the oven for 10 minutes. Take them out and allow them to cool, then remove the skins. Leave the nuts whole, or roughly chop them -- however you prefer. Set aside.
- Bring the red wine vinegar and 1/2 cup of water to a healthy simmer. Add the raisins

and turn down the heat to low. Cover, then cook for 10 minutes. Turn off the heat and allow the raisins to sit in the vinegar solution for an additional 20 minutes. Drain the raisins and set them aside.

- Bring a pot of water to a rolling boil, then add enough kosher salt to make the water taste like the sea. Add the orzo to the pot and cook until al dente (for me, this was consistently 2 minutes less than the bag recommended). Drain the orzo, transfer to a bowl, and stir in a bit of olive oil -- just enough so that the pasta doesn't stick. Allow the orzo to cool for 20 to 30 minutes.
- Make the dressing: Add the lime juice, rice wine vinegar, and champagne vinegar to a small bowl. Whisk in a little pinch of kosher salt. Add the sesame oil and 2 tablespoons of olive oil. Whisk the dressing to emulsify the oil, then set aside.
- Clean and thinly slice the whites and light greens of the scallions. Mince the chives.
- Stir the red pepper flakes into the orzo. Add the hazelnuts, raisins, scallions, and chives. Fold in the dressing. Stir in the sea salt. Using a fork, break up the goat cheese, then crumble it into the bowl and lightly fold to combine. Serve chilled or at room temperature. Author's Note: If you are eating the salad fresh, I think 1/2 cup of dressing is sufficient. I usually save the remaining 1/4 cup for just before serving, especially if I make the salad ahead of time. But add the dressing bit by bit, then stop when it tastes right to you.

---

78. Oysters With A Champagne Cucumber Mignonette

Serving: Makes at least 2 dozen oysters | Prep: | Cook: | Ready in:

Ingredients

- oysters on the half shell
- 1/4 cup champagne vinegar

- 1 tablespoon shallots, finely minced
- 4 teaspoons cucumber, peeled, seeded, and finely minced
- 1/4 teaspoon kosher salt
- pinch of pepper
- 2 tablespoons champagne

Direction

- Combine the vinegar, shallots, cucumber, salt, and pepper in a small dish. Place in the fridge so it chills.
- Shuck the oysters and place on the half shell (or smile pretty for the fishmonger and ask him to do it for you).
- Just before serving, remove the mignonette from the fridge and add the champagne.
- Serve the oysters with the mignonette on the side.
- Add a small spoon of mignonette to each oyster and slurp!

79. Pan Seared Pork Chops With Blueberry Herb Sauce

Serving: Serves 4 | Prep: | Cook: | Ready in:

Ingredients

- For the blueberry herb sauce:
- 1 cup blueberries (about 3/4 pint)
- 1/4 cup cilantro, roughly chopped
- 1/4 cup parsley, roughly chopped
- 1   shallot, finely chopped
- 3   cloves garlic, finely chopped
- 1 teaspoon kosher salt
- 1/2 teaspoon freshly cracked black pepper
- 1/2 teaspoon crushed red pepper flakes
- 1 1/2 tablespoons Champagne vinegar
- 1/4 cup extra-virgin olive oil
- For the pork chops:
- 4   bone-in pork chops, about 10 ounces each
- 2 tablespoons canola or vegetable oil
- 1 1/2 tablespoons salt

- 1 1/2 tablespoons freshly ground pepper
- 1 tablespoon butter

Direction

- Using a mortar and pestle (or a medium-sized bowl and the back of a wooden spoon), muddle the berries, cilantro, and parsley until nearly all of the berries have burst.
- Add the shallot, garlic, salt, black pepper, crushed red pepper, Champagne vinegar, and olive oil, and mix to incorporate. Taste and adjust seasonings. Cover and set aside until ready to use (at least 30 minutes, or up to 3 days in the refrigerator.)
- Pat pork chops dry with paper towels.
- In a cast iron or other heavy-bottomed skillet, heat the vegetable oil over medium-high heat. While the skillet is heating, season the pork chops with salt and pepper. (They should be well-covered in the seasonings, including the sides and fat.)
- Once the oil in the skillet is hot, add the pork chops and cook them for 8 minutes, flipping the chops every minute to achieve an even, golden color. (Note: You may need to work in batches if the pork chops don't all fit in your skillet—they will not brown properly if overcrowded.)
- Add the butter to the skillet. Once melted, spoon the butter over the tops of the pork chops, remove them from the heat, and let them rest for 3 minutes. Serve immediately, with the blueberry herb sauce on top of the chops or on the side.

80. Pasta With Fried Artichoke Chips, Pancetta, Roasted Tomatoes And Lemon Breadcrumbs

Serving: Serves 4 | Prep: | Cook: | Ready in:

Ingredients

- 1 pint container of grape tomatoes
- 2 tablespoons minced garlic
- 2 tablespoons olive oil
- 4 jumbo artichokes
- juice of one lemon
- 6 - 8 cups water
- 1/2 cup white wine
- 2 tablespoons citrus champagne vinegar
- 3 garlic cloves, smashed
- few sprigs fresh thyme
- few sprigs fresh mint
- 4 ounces pancetta
- 2/3 cup fresh bread crumbs from day-old bread
- zest from 1 medium lemon
- 1/8 cup chopped parsley
- 2 tablespoons parmesan cheese, grated
- salt and pepper to taste
- 1 package spaghetti noodles (or enough for 4 people)

Direction

- Make the roasted tomatoes: Preheat oven to 275F. Slice tomatoes in half and toss with garlic and olive oil. Salt and pepper to taste. Place them on a baking sheet, all turned with the cut side facing up. Roast for approximately 1 to 1 1/2 hour or until they are somewhat shriveled up and a little dry to the touch. Don't roast them until they are complete shriveled up or the pasta dish will taste a little dry. Set aside.
- Prep and pre-cook the artichokes: Snap off all the leaves from the artichokes and discard. Trim the base with a paring knife until smooth and all dark green leaf spots where the leaves were attached are removed. Remove the choke with the paring knife and a grapefruit spoon. In order to keep the artichoke bottoms from turning brown, soak each artichoke bottom in lemon water until ready to cook.
- Bring the water, lemon juice, white wine and champagne vinegar to a boil. Add the thyme, mint, garlic, 1 Tablespoon of salt and artichoke bottoms. Cook the artichoke bottoms until just tender. Remove from the acidulated water and

dry. When cool enough to handle, remove any last part of the choke with a grapefruit spoon, and slice into thin slices.
- Add enough water to the acidulated water for the pasta and bring back to a boil. Add the pasta and cook according the package directions.
- Chop the pancetta into 1/2" pieces and fry until crispy. Drain and set aside. Pour out the bacon grease.
- Make the lemon breadcrumbs: sauté the bread crumbs in 1 Tablespoon olive oil over medium heat for about 3-4 minutes until just starting to change color. Add the lemon zest and 1/8 teaspoon each of salt and pepper. Sauté another 4-5 minutes until crispy and a deep golden brown.
- Heat oil in the same pan used to fry the pancetta. Lightly salt and pepper the artichoke slices and dust with Wondra flour. When the oil is hot enough to make them sizzle, fry the artichoke slices - about 4 minutes per side - until they are a light brown and a little crispy.
- Assemble the pasta: toss the artichokes, roasted tomatoes, pancetta, lemon breadcrumbs and chopped parsley with the pasta. Top with a little parmesan cheese.

81. Petit Champagne Layer Cakes

Serving: Makes 12 | Prep: | Cook: |Ready in:

Ingredients

- Champagne Angel Food Cakes
- 1 cup Cake Flour
- 1 1/2 cups Confectioner's Sugar
- 1 1/2 cups Egg Whites
- 1 1/2 teaspoons Cream of Tartar
- 1 cup Granulated Sugar + more for coating pan
- 1/4 cup Champagne
- 2 tablespoons Unrefined Coconut Oil (for coating pan)
- Champagne Swiss Meringue Buttercream

- 6 Egg Whites
- 1 3/4 cups Granulated Sugar
- 1 teaspoon Salt
- 1/2 teaspoon Cream of Tartar
- 1/2 tablespoon Vanilla Extract
- 32 tablespoons Butter, softened
- 1/2 cup Champagne

Direction

- Champagne Angel Food Cakes
- Grease a popover pan with unrefined coconut oil (regular will do in a pinch). Coat with granulated sugar by placing a small spoonful in the bottom of each popover cup and then rotating pan around until all sides of each cup are coated.
- Preheat oven to 375 degrees.
- Sift flour and confectioner's sugar together three times for best texture.
- Combine egg whites, cream of tartar and salt and beat until foamy.
- Very gradually add in granulated sugar, beating with hand mixer or stand mixer until meringue holds stiff peaks.
- In a small sauce pan, boil down champagne to ½ tsp.
- Let cool and gently fold in meringue along with vanilla.
- Sprinkle the flour/sugar mixture over meringue and fold just until well combined.
- Using a heaping ¼ C measure portion the batter into popover pan. Cups should be approximately 7/8 full.
- Bake at 375 for 18-20 minutes or until toothpick inserted comes out clean.
- Turn popover pan upside down onto cooling rack and leave alone until completely cool. Using a toothpick, gently release any part of cake stuck to inside of cup and pull cake out with a fork.
- Champagne Swiss Meringue Buttercream
- Fill a small saucepan with about 2 inches of water and bring to a simmer. Rest the metal bowl from a stand mixer on top of the saucepan, making sure the bottom does not touch the water.

- In the bowl beat the egg whites, sugar, salt and cream of tartar. Continue beating as the mixture heats over the simmering water.
- When egg white mixture reaches 120 degrees, remove from heat and place bowl into the stand mixture fitting with whisk attachment. Beat until stiff peaks form, and meringue is glossy. Let meringue cool completely.
- Once cool, begin beating mixture on medium high setting and add vanilla and then butter, one tablespoon at a time.
- Beat for a few more minutes until butter is completely incorporated and frosting begins to firm up slightly.
- Carefully pour in champagne in a thin stream while beater is going. Once champagne is fully incorporated scrape down bowl with spatula and continue to beat frosting until fluffy, but firm.
- Using a piece of floss, cut each cake into three equal layers. Using a pastry bag with ¼ inch tip, frost each layer, top with a bright red strawberry, pour a glass of that champagne you have left over on the counter and have a toast.

82. Pink Champagne Cake

Serving: Serves 12 | Prep: 0hours30mins | Cook: 1hours0mins | Ready in:

Ingredients

- Cake
- 3 cups cake flour
- 1 tablespoon baking powder
- 1/2 teaspoon salt
- 5 large egg whites, at room temperature
- 1 cup pink Champagne, at room temperature
- 2 teaspoons vanilla extract
- 2 teaspoons vegetable oil
- 2 cups granulated sugar
- 1 cup (2 sticks) unsalted butter, at room temperature

- 1 drop pink food coloring (more for darker pink)
- Pink Champagne Buttercream Frosting
- 1 3/4 cups (3 1/2 sticks) unsalted butter, at room temperature
- 8 cups confectioners' sugar, sifted
- 4 tablespoons pink Champagne
- 1 teaspoon vanilla extract
- 1 drop pink food coloring (more for darker pink)

Direction

- For the cake, place a rack in the center of the oven, and preheat the oven to 350°F. Grease and flour three 8-inch layer pans. Shake out the excess flour, and set the pans aside.
- Place the flour, baking powder, and salt in a medium-size bowl, and sift to combine well. Set aside.
- Place the egg whites, Champagne, vanilla, and oil in a large mixing bowl, and whisk by hand until well blended. Set aside.
- Place the sugar and butter in a large bowl, and beat with an electric mixer on medium speed until creamy and light, 3 to 4 minutes. Add the flour mixture and the egg white mixture alternately, beginning and ending with the dry ingredients. Stir in the pink coloring. Divide the batter between the prepared pans, and place the pans in the oven.
- Bake until the cakes just pull back from the sides of the pans, 23 to 27 minutes. Remove the pans from the oven, and place them on a wire rack to cool for 10 minutes. Run a knife around the edges of each pan, give each cake a gentle shake, then invert it once and then again onto the rack to cool completely, right side up, 30 minutes.
- While the cakes are cooling, prepare the frosting. Place the butter in a large mixing bowl, and beat on medium speed until creamy and smooth, 1 minute. Add 6 cups of the confectioners' sugar and the champagne and vanilla. Blend on medium speed until smooth. Add the remaining confectioners' sugar, adding what you need to make the frosting

thick but spreadable. Increase the mixer speed to medium-high, add the pink coloring, and beat until the frosting is fluffy, 30 seconds.
- To assemble the cake, place 1 layer on a cake plate. Spread about 3/4 cup of the frosting to the edges. Place a second layer on top and repeat. Place the third layer on top, and frost the top and sides of the cake with the remaining frosting. Garnish with white chocolate shavings, sliced strawberries, coconut, or edible rose petals if desired, depending on the occasion. Slice and serve.

---

83. Pom Fizz

Serving: Makes 1 drink | Prep: 0hours5mins | Cook: 2hours0mins | Ready in:

Ingredients

- Pomegranate Syrup
- 4 cups 100% pomegranate juice
- Pom Fizz
- 1 tablespoon Pomegranate Syrup
- 4 ounces Prosecco or other sparkling white wine
- 4 fresh pomegranate arils/seeds

Direction

- Pomegranate Syrup
- Add the juice to a large saucepan and set it over medium-low heat, stirring occasionally, until it reduces to a syrup, about 2 hours. Store in a covered container in the refrigerator.
- Pom Fizz
- Add the Pomegranate Syrup to a champagne flute or coupe, then pour in the sparkling wine and float in a few pomegranate arils.

84. Potato (Plus) Salad With Champagne Honeydew Mignonette

Serving: Serves 10, or fewer with leftovers | Prep: | Cook: | Ready in:

Ingredients

- 3 pounds red or Yukon gold, or fingerling potatoes, well washed
- 1 tablespoon sea or kosher salt
- 1 pound French style green beans
- 1 red onion, fine dice
- 1 cup kalamata olives, rough chopped
- 1 cup Feta cheese, crumbled
- 6 ounces champagne vinegar
- 1/2 cup puréed honeydew melon
- 2 shallots, minced (3 if they're small)
- 1 generous tablespoon fresh tarragon, chopped
- Sea or kosher salt and pepper to taste
- Pinch red pepper flakes

Direction

- Cut the potatoes into 1/2" cubes, no smaller. Place them in a pot with cold water to cover and add a tablespoon salt. Bring to a boil over medium-high heat, then reduce to an active simmer. Cook just until they can be easily pierced with a sharp knife, about 10-15 minutes. Drain into a colander, then set the colander in your original pan and place both under cold running water, gently moving the potatoes around with your hands until they are completely cool through to the center. Remove the colander, and leave the potatoes to continue draining. When finished, transfer them to a large mixing bowl. Retain the colander for the beans.
- Refill the same pot with water and bring to a boil. While waiting, wash your beans. Set a bowl of ice water right next to the stove. When the water comes to a boil, add the beans all at once. As soon as the water returns to the boil, set a timer for 2 minutes. You only want to blanch the beans long enough to break down a bit of their toughness, but not their wonderful crunch. After 2 minutes, use tongs to lift the beans out of the pot and drop into the ice water. Let them cool completely through. When ready, transfer them to the colander in the sink and allow to drain.
- Meanwhile, dice the red onion and add it to the bowl containing the potatoes. Chop the green beans into 2-inch lengths and add them to the same bowl. Drain and roughly chop the Kalamatas and add them also. Add the Feta cheese. Gently toss to blend using a rubber spatula.
- Using a mortar and pestle (a wooden one works best), pound the chunks of melon to a juicy pulp. Alternatively, dice them very fine with a knife, then smash on your board using a fork. Transfer every bit of pulp and juice to a small bowl. Add the champagne vinegar, shallots, tarragon, salt and pepper to taste and a pinch of red pepper flakes. Whisk to blend, pour over salad contents and gently toss together. Allow salad to sit for 15 minutes, then gently toss once more. Let sit for 15 minutes more, toss again, and taste for seasoning, adjusting as you wish. Refrigerate until ready to pack up and go. Don't be surprised if you find yourself dipping into it for *just one more taste.*

85. Refreshing French 75

Serving: Serves 1 | Prep: | Cook: | Ready in:

Ingredients

- 1 ounce gin
- 1/2 ounce simple syrup (I made my own but that's up to you)
- 1/2 ounce fresh squeezed lemon juice
- Brut Champagne or a dry sparkling white wine
- Twist of lemon (garnish)

Direction

- Combine gin, simple syrup, and lemon juice in a cocktail shaker filled with ice.
- Shake until well chilled and strain into a glass.
- Top with Champagne and garnish with a lemon twist to serve.

---

86. Roasted Kumquat Trifle

Serving: Serves 4 to 6, depending on serving size (you may have some cake leftover) | Prep: | Cook: | Ready in:

Ingredients

- 18 ounces kumquats, sliced
- 4 tablespoons Champagne vinegar, more or less to taste
- 2/3 cup plus 4 tablespoons granulated sugar, divided
- 1/2 teaspoon ground ginger (optional)
- White Chocolate Whipped Cream (https://food52.com/recipes...)
- 4 tablespoons butter
- 4 egg yolks
- 2 teaspoons vanilla extract
- 4 egg whites
- Pinch salt
- 3/4 cup cake flour

Direction

- Preheat oven to 350° F.
- Macerate the sliced kumquats in the Champagne vinegar and 2 tablespoons of sugar. Feel free to layer in (or leave out) the ground ginger. This mixture can sit for just 30 minutes or up to 4 hours before you are ready to serve, depending on your time constraints or flavor preferences. Kumquats don't expel as much juice as their other peeled cousins, so once everything is in a bowl together, I'd give it a good mix and mash with my hands.
- Since it needs to chill for a few hours before you whip it, this is a good point to make the white chocolate and heavy cream mixture for the whipped cream. Store it in the refrigerator after it has cooled to await whipping.
- Line a 10-inch cake pan with buttered parchment paper. Measure out all of your cake ingredients (including the remaining sugar).
- Melt the butter and set aside to cool.
- Gradually beat 2/3 cup of sugar into the egg yolks, add the vanilla, and continue beating for several minutes until the mixture is thick, pale yellow, and forms ribbons when you drizzle it.
- Beat the egg whites and salt together in a separate bowl until soft peaks are formed; sprinkle on the remaining 2 tablespoons of the sugar and beat until stiff peaks are formed. Scoop 1/4 of the egg whites over the top of the egg yolks and sugar mixture. Sift 1/4 of the cake flour on top, then delicately fold in until partially blended. Then add 1/3 of the remaining egg whites, sift in 1/3 of the remaining flour, fold until partially blended, and repeat. Then add the last of each and half of the tepid, melted butter. When partially blended, fold in the rest of the butter but omit the milky residue at the bottom of the pan. Do not over mix; the egg whites must retain as much volume as possible.
- Turn the batter into the prepared cake pan. Spread the kumquats onto a baking sheet. Set the cake in the middle level of your preheated oven for 30 to 35 minutes, along with the macerated kumquats. The cake is done when it has puffed, is lightly brown, and has just begun to show a faint line of shrinkage from the edge of the pan. (I think this last indicator is really key; it's a helpful visual cue to look for.) The kumquats can come out at the same time; you want them to have the consistency of a chunky compote or spread—they won't be as syrupy or liquidy as some trifle fillings.
- While the cake and kumquats are in the oven, whip your premade heavy cream and white chocolate mixture to preferred consistency.
- Remove the cake and the kumquats from oven and let stand in the pan for 6 to 8 minutes. The cake will sink slightly and shrink more from

the edges of the pan. Run a knife around the edge of the pan, and reverse on cake rack (or plate, in my case), giving the pan a sharp little jerk to dislodge the cake. Allow to cool for an hour or so. The kumquats can be served room temperature or chilled.

- Assemble your individual trifles in a casual way: While you could cut the cake into uniform cubes, I'd tear it into a mismatched group. Toss about 4 or 5 cubes into each dessert bowl, top with a healthy dollop (or two) of white chocolate whipped cream, and as little or as much roasted kumquats as you'd like.

87. Roasted Pear And Rainbow Chard Salad

Serving: Serves 4 | Prep: | Cook: |Ready in:

Ingredients

- For the vinaigrette:
- 2 tablespoons freshly squeezed lemon juice
- 4 teaspoons Champagne vinegar
- 1 teaspoon Dijon mustard
- 1 pinch sea salt
- 1/3 cup extra-virgin olive oil
- For the salad:
- 1 tablespoon extra-virgin olive oil
- 1 tablespoon Champagne vinegar
- 4   small, firm pears (I went with a mix of Green Anjou and Bosc here)
- Sea salt, to taste
- Black pepper, to taste
- 1 bunch rainbow chard, stems trimmed and roughly chopped
- 1/2 cup chèvre
- 4   lemon wedges, for serving

Direction

- For the vinaigrette:
- In a small bowl, whisk the lemon juice, vinegar, Dijon, and sea salt to combine. When

the mixture is well combined, slowly drizzle in the olive oil, whisking vigorously until vinaigrette is nicely emulsified.

- For the salad:
- Preheat oven to 375° F. In a small bowl, whisk together the olive oil and Champagne vinegar.
- Halve pears and carefully cut out the core. Set pears with sliced side facing up on a rimmed baking sheet. Drizzle olive oil mixture over pears and sprinkle each with sea salt and pepper.
- Slide the baking sheet into the oven. Roast for 8 minutes, then use tongs to flip the pears, and return them to the oven for 6 to 8 more minutes, or until the edges are golden and the pears are easily pierced with a fork. Set aside to cool.
- In a large bowl, toss the greens with half of the vinaigrette. Crumble in chèvre and toss gently. Divide greens between four plates, add 2 pear halves to each, and drizzle with the remaining dressing. Finish salads with a pinch of sea salt and a liberal sprinkle of black pepper, and garnish with a lemon wedge.

88. Rosemary & Clementine Champagne Cocktail

Serving: Makes 1 drink | Prep: | Cook: |Ready in:

Ingredients

- Rosemary Simple Syrup
- 1/2 cup Water
- 1/2 cup Sugar
- 3 sprigs Rosemary
- Cocktail
- 1 tablespoon Rosemary Simple Syrup
- 1 ounce Fresh Squeezed Clementine Juice
- Champagne

Direction

- In a small pan over high heat add the sugar and water. Keep stirring until the sugar is completely dissolved and turn it off. Add the fresh rosemary sprigs and let them steep in there until the syrup is cooled to touch.

- In a champagne glass add the simple syrup, clementine juice, and top it off with cold champagne. I like to add a little rosemary sprig on the top for garnish.

89. Rosy Champagne

Serving: Serves 1 | Prep: | Cook: |Ready in:

Ingredients

- Rose and lemon simple syrup
- 2/3 cup water
- 1 lemon, zest and juice
- 1/4 cup sugar
- 1/4 cup Rooh Afza syrup (Hamdard brand)
- 1 1/2 tablespoons rose water
- Drink
- 2 tablespoons rose and lemon simple syrup
- 1 cup dry champagne
- thinly sliced lemon to garnish

Direction

- For the simple syrup: combine all ingredients in a small saucepan and bring to a boil. Remove from heat and gently stir to dissolve all sugar. Allow to cool, strain, and chill.
- Put two tablespoons of the simple syrup in a glass, and top with champagne. Garnish with lemon slices and sip prettily.

90. SCALLOPS IN CHAMPAGNE CREAM SAUCE WITH TRUFFLE SALT

Serving: Serves 2 - 3 | Prep: | Cook: |Ready in:

Ingredients

- 4 pieces scallops per person
- 3 pieces medium shallots (1.5 oz)
- 1 cup white Champagne
- 1 cup heavy cream
- Freshly ground black pepper
- Splash Olive oil or butter for sautéeing scallops
- large pinches Sea salt with truffles
- 7 ounces fresh pasta per person
- Olive oil and lemon juice to taste

Direction

- In a large pot, start the water boiling for the pasta. If it comes to a boil before you are ready to make the pasta, simply lower the heat and allow to very slowly simmer until the sauce and scallops are nearly cooked.
- Rinse the scallops then pat dry with paper towels.
- Peel, trim and mince the shallots.
- Place the minced shallots with the champagne in a small, heavy bottom saucepan and, over medium heat, cook until the champagne is almost (but not quite) evaporated, stirring often. There should be just a tablespoon or two of champagne left in the pan.
- Lower the heat under the saucepan and add the cream, stirring, and allow to cook just a few minutes until slightly thickened. Season with freshly ground black pepper.
- Meanwhile, when the champagne is partly evaporated, start the scallops. Heat a skillet or frying pan over medium heat and add just enough olive oil or butter to grease the bottom and, when hot, add the scallops and allow to cook, turning occasionally, until golden and crispy on both sides and cooked through (you will see the scallops turn from translucent to opaque white all the way through), lowering the heat if the scallops look browned enough on the top and bottom but don't appear cooked completely through. This should take up to 5 minutes per side for very thick scallops.
- If the sauce is done before the scallops are cooked through, simply turn off the heat

- under the sauce and then very gently reheat the sauce when ready to serve, if necessary.
- Cook the fresh pasta (which only takes 3 minutes or so) in salted boiling water then drain. Place the pasta in a bowl and add a few glugs of olive oil, the juice of about half a lemon or to taste and a good grinding of black pepper. Toss and dress the plates with a serving of pasta each.
- Place a few spoonfuls of the Champagne Sauce on the pasta then place the scallops on top of the sauce. Sprinkle the scallops with Truffle Salt and serve accompanied by a glass with extra sauce if desired. Serve with a glass of chilled Champagne.
- This recipe easily makes enough sauce to serve 4 people. I served 2 and had sauce leftover for another dish the following lunch.

91. Seven Bean Salad

Serving: Serves 8-10 | Prep: | Cook: | Ready in:

Ingredients

- Lemon Dijon Dressing
- 6 tablespoons olive oil
- 3 tablespoons champagne vinegar
- 1 teaspoon Dijon mustard
- 1   small garlic clove, minced
- 1 teaspoon mustard seeds
- 1/2 teaspoon lemon zest
- 1/4 teaspoon freshly ground black pepper
- Seven Bean Salad
- 2 cups fresh green beans, ends snipped
- 1½ cups frozen edamame, thawed
- 2 cups snow peas
- 1 cup fresh green peas
- 1½ cups canned chickpeas, rinsed and drained
- 1½ cups baby lima beans, rinsed and drained
- 1½ cups white (cannellini) beans, rinsed and drained
- 1 tablespoon chopped fresh flat-leaf parsley

- 2 teaspoons fresh thyme
- 1 teaspoon lemon zest
- 1/4 teaspoon kosher salt, or more to taste

Direction

- For the Lemon Dijon dressing, in a food processor or blender, combine olive oil, champagne vinegar, Dijon mustard, garlic, mustard seeds, lemon zest, salt and pepper. Pulse 2-3 times, until well combines. Set aside.
- For the salad, bring a medium pot of water to a boil over high heat. Add green beans and edamame. Turn heat to low and cook 1 minute. Add snow peas and fresh green peas and continue cooking 1 minute more. Drain and immediately plunge into a bowl of ice water to stop cooking. Once cold, drain again and dry out completely. Place in a large bowl along with chickpeas, lima beans, white beans, parsley, thyme, lemon zest and salt. Pour dressing over salad, toss well and refrigerate covered until ready to serve.

92. Shades Of Green Chopped Salad

Serving: Serves 2 to 3 | Prep: 0hours0mins | Cook: 0hours0mins | Ready in:

Ingredients

- Chive dressing
- 1   small clove garlic
- 2 tablespoons Champagne vinegar
- 1 teaspoon crème fraîche
- 1 tablespoon honey
- 1 tablespoon chopped chives
- 2 tablespoons extra-virgin olive oil
- 1 pinch sea salt and black pepper, plus more to taste
- Salad
- 1   Granny Smith apple, chopped
- 1   Hass avocado, chopped
- 1 tablespoon freshly squeezed lemon juice
- 1/2   English cucumber, chopped

- 1/4 cup chopped pistachios
- 1/4 cup golden raisins
- 1/3 cup crumbled gorgonzola cheese, room temperature
- 1 pinch salt and black pepper, plus more to taste
- 2 tablespoons chopped chives, for garnish (optional)

Direction

- Chive dressing
- In a blender, add in the garlic, Champagne vinegar, crème fraîche, honey, chives, salt, and pepper. Blend until combined.
- With the blender still on, through the top, stream in the olive oil. Blend until combined. Taste for salt and pepper. Set aside.
- Salad
- Toss the apple and avocado in the lemon juice so they don't oxidize. Then, combine all of the ingredients in a bowl and toss with the chive dressing. You may not have to use all of the dressing—I don't like mine too wet. Season with salt and pepper to taste. Garnish with some chopped chives. This salad can be made up to 3 to 4 hours in advance. If you are making the salad in advance add in the room temperature gorgonzola when you serve the salad.

93. Shades Of Green Chopped Salad

Serving: Serves 2-3 | Prep: | Cook: | Ready in:

Ingredients

- for the chive dressing
- 1   small clove garlic
- 2 tablespoons Champagne vinegar
- 1 teaspoon creme fraiche
- 1 tablespoon honey
- 1 tablespoon chopped chives
- 2 tablespoons extra-virgin olive oil
- sea salt and black pepper, to taste

- for the chopped salad
- 1   Granny Smith apple, chopped
- 1   Hass avocado, chopped
- 1 tablespoon freshly squeezed lemon juice
- 1/2 english cucumber, chopped
- 1/4 cup chopped pistachios
- 1/4 cup green raisins
- 1/4-1/2 cups (depending on how much cheese you like in your salad) crumbled gorgonzola cheese, at room temperature
- chive dressing (recipe above)
- salt and black pepper, if necessary
- chopped chives, for garnish, optional

Direction

- For the chive dressing
- In a blender, add in the garlic, Champagne vinegar, crème fraiche, honey, chives, salt, and pepper. Blend until combined.
- With the blender still on, through the top, stream in the olive oil. Blend until combined. Taste for salt and pepper. Set aside.
- For the chopped salad
- Toss the apple and avocado in the lemon juice so they don't oxidize. Then, combine all of the ingredients in a bowl and toss with the chive dressing. You may not have to use all of the dressing, it depends on how you like your salad. I don't like mine too wet. If necessary, add extra salt and pepper. Garnish with some chopped chives. This salad can be made up to 3-4 hours in advance. If you are making the salad in advance add in the room temperature gorgonzola when you serve the salad.

94. Shredded Zucchini Salad

Serving: Serves 4 | Prep: | Cook: | Ready in:

Ingredients

- 4   zucchini, unpeeled
- 2 cups cherry tomatoes
- 1 cup micro radish (or other micro greens)

- 1/2 cup basil
- 1 tablespoon champagne vinegar
- 1 teaspoon Dijon mustard
- 1 tablespoon fresh lemon juice
- 2 tablespoons olive oil
- sea salt, pepper

Direction

- Wash and trim the zucchini (no need to peel). Grate the zucchini on a box grater or process in a food processor with the shredding attachment. Toss the zucchini with 1/2 tsp salt in a colander. Set aside to drain for 30 minutes.
- Whisk together the champagne vinegar, mustard, lemon juice, and olive oil.
- Wash and halve or quarter the cherry tomatoes.
- Drain the zucchini and squeeze out all of the extra liquid. You can either wrap up the zucchini in a clean kitchen towel and wring it dry or just use your hands for the task.
- Toss the zucchini, cherry tomatoes, and vinaigrette together. Adjust the seasoning, adding more lemon juice or vinegar. It should taste bright and refreshing, not dull or chalky. Add more salt, if needed.
- Chill for at least 20 minutes before serving.
- Chiffonade the basil: stack the leaves like a deck of cards, roll them up into a cigar (or yoga mat) and slice into 1/4-inch thick ribbons.
- To serve, portion out 1 cup of the salad on each plate. Scatter micro radish and basil over the salad and drizzle with additional olive oil.
- Store in the fridge for up to two days.
- Note: Substitute white balsamic, white wine, or red wine vinegar for the champagne vinegar, if necessary. The zucchini should be pretty salty after draining so you may not need to add additional salt to the salad.

95. Shrimp Orzo Salad

Serving: Serves 6-8 | Prep: | Cook: |Ready in:

Ingredients

- Shrimp Preparation
- 1 pound uncooked shrimp (31-40ct), thawed, de-veined, tails removed
- 2 tablespoons extra virgin olive oil or grape seed oil
- 1/2 teaspoon sea salt
- 1/4 teaspoon pepper
- Orzo Prepartation
- 2 cups uncooked orzo
- 2 cloves of garlic minced
- 1 large red pepper, finely diced, about 2 cups
- 1/2 large red onion, finely diced, about 1 1/2 cups
- 1 tablespoon olive oil
- 1 teaspoon kosher salt, divided
- 1/2 teaspoon ground black pepper, divided
- 2 tablespoons basil chiffonade
- 1/2 cup fresh parsley, chopped
- 5 tablespoons extra virgin olive oil
- 1 tablespoon champagne vineagar
- 2 tablespoons fresh lemon juice
- 2 teaspoons ground cumin
- 1 teaspoon ground ginger

Direction

- Shrimp Preparation
- Pre-heat the oven to 400 degrees, adjust oven rack to the second rung from the top
- Line a large rimmed baking sheet with parchment paper (do not grease the pan)
- Rinse shrimp. They should be thawed, de-veined and tails removed
- In a medium bowl, with your hands, gently toss the shrimp with the olive oil, salt and pepper.
- Evenly spread the shrimp out on the prepared baking sheet.
- Bake the shrimp for about 4-5 minutes or until pink. Do not over bake!

- Remove from the oven and cool to room temperature.
- Orzo Preparation
- Bring a large saucepan filled with salted water to boil.
- Add the Orzo and cook until al dente, between 6-8 min (I am at altitude so can take me longer to cook pasta).
- While the orzo is cooking, finely dice the garlic, red pepper, and red onion and set aside.
- The orzo is probably done by the time you dice the garlic, peppers and onions. Drain the orzo well and set aside in a large bowl to cool.
- After the orzo has cooled for about 5 min, add 1 TB of olive oil and mix in with a wooden spoon.
- Next, chiffonade the basil and chop the parsley.
- Stir in the garlic peppers, onions, basil, parsley, 1/2 of the salt and pepper and the shrimp.
- For the dressing, combine 5 TB olive oil, 1 TB champagne vinegar, 2 TB fresh lemon juice, 2 tsp cumin, 1 tsp ginger, 1/2 tsp salt, and 1/2 tsp pepper. Whisk until well combined.
- Fold gently into pasta.
- Serve immediately, or chill for a few hours or overnight.

96. Smoked Trout Salad With Peaches And Wasabi

Serving: Serves 4 | Prep: | Cook: | Ready in:

Ingredients

- Champagne Wasabi Vinaigrette
- 1/3 cup champagne vinegar
- 2/3 cup blood orange flavored olive oil
- 1   lemon, juice & pulp
- 1 teaspoon wasabi
- 2 teaspoons Dijon mustard
- 1   clove garlic minced

- 1 tablespoon Marinade au Poivre
- 2 teaspoons vidalia onion & peach hot sauce
- 1 teaspoon Hara Masala (corriander sauce found in Indian markets)
- 1-2 teaspoons sugar (to taste)
- freshly ground black pepper
- Salad with Smoked Trout and Toasted Pecans
- 1/2 cup toasted pecans
- 2   green onions sliced
- 1   orange sweet pepper diced
- 1-2   Peaches or nectarines roasted on the grill
- 1 bunch watercress or arugula
- 1   fennel bulb shaved thinly
- 3/4 cup smoked trout (flaked)
- 1/2 pint seared scallops

Direction

- Champagne Wasabi Vinaigrette
- In a small bowl mix the vinaigrette. The essential idea is the play of the wasabi, hot sauce and fruit flavors with the champagne vinaigrette. There are many possible variations but this one was memorable. Improvise if you don't have one of the specialty flavorings like Marinade au Poivre or Hara Masala.
- Salad with Smoked Trout and Toasted Pecans
- Sear the scallops on the grill. Slice the peaches and wrap in foil. Place on the grill for about 10 minutes. Cut away the woody part of the fennel and discard. Shave the remaining fennel with a mandolin. Wash the cress or arugula and arrange make a bed on each serving plate. Toss the fennel with the vinaigrette and spoon over the greens. Flake the trout and add the peaches and pecans.

97. Smokey Grilled Potato And Corn Salad

Serving: Serves 4-6 | Prep: | Cook: | Ready in:

Ingredients

- 2 pounds small red potatoes, scrubbed

- 4   scallions, trimmed
- 3   ears of corn, husked and silks removed
- 2   cloves of garlic - not peeled - skewered on a wooden stick
- 2-3 tablespoons olive oil
- 3/4 cup mayonnaise
- 1 - 2 teaspoons smoked paprika
- 1/2 teaspoon cumin
- 3 tablespoons Champagne vinegar
- 1 teaspoon lemon zest
- 1   bunch watercress, chopped

Direction

- To pre-cook the potatoes, place them whole in a stock pot of boiling salted water and cook for 15 - 20 minutes until they are just tender (this will depend greatly on the size of your potatoes). Drain and cool slightly so you can handle them. Cut in half or in quarters - depending on the size of your potatoes (but big enough that they can sit on your grill grates and not fall through).
- Light your grill to medium high. Brush your potatoes, corn, scallions, and garlic with olive oil and season with salt and pepper. Grill the potatoes until they have nice grill marks - but they should be cooked through in step one.
- Grill the corn about 5 minutes - until it is nicely browned and charred in some spots. Grill the scallions about 2 minutes per side - until browned. Cook the garlic skewers on a cooler area of the grill, turning frequently, until the clove is softened but does not burn. (Depending on the size of the clove - 8-10 minutes).
- Place the potatoes in a bowl. Cut the corn off the cob and chop the scallions and place them in the bowl with the potatoes.
- Make the dressing: Peel and crush the garlic into a paste. Mix it with the mayo, (1-2 teaspoons - see headnote) smoked paprika, cumin, champagne vinegar, and lemon zest. Season with salt and pepper.
- Add the watercress to the potato mixture and pour the dressing over (see headnote - first start with half and add more to reach your

desired creaminess) and fold in gently. Taste for seasoning. Can be served slightly warm, at room temp, or chilled.

98. Sparkling Apple Brandy Cocktail

Serving: Serves 1 | Prep: | Cook: |Ready in:

Ingredients

- 1.5 ounces Brandy
- 2/5 tablespoon Apple Cider
- 1 cup Chilled Brut Champagne

Direction

- In a cocktail shaker, combine brandy and apple cider. Add ice and shake vigorously for about 30 seconds.
- Strain into Champagne flute and top with Champagne.
- Garnish with a cinnamon stick, if desired.

99. Sparkling Negroni

Serving: Serves 2 | Prep: | Cook: |Ready in:

Ingredients

- 2 ounces Campari
- 2 ounces sweet vermouth
- 2 ounces gin
- sparkling wine, prosecco or champagne, to finish

Direction

- Fill a cocktail shaker with ice and add in your Campari, sweet vermouth and gin. Stir vigorously for 5 seconds, then strain and pour over chilled glasses (they can also be filled with ice or not, this is up to you). Top with sparkling wine, Prosecco or champagne and enjoy.

100. Squealing Purple B

Serving: Serves 4 | Prep: | Cook: | Ready in:

Ingredients

- 4 ounces tequila
- 1 ounce lime juice
- 1/2 ounce agave syrup
- 1/2 ounce acai pulp
- 2 ounces champagne
- lime slices for garnish

Direction

- Shake tequila, lime, agave and acai vigorously with ice. Strain into glasses and top with champagne. Garnish with lime.

101. Strawberry Basil Champagne Cocktail

Serving: Serves 1 | Prep: | Cook: | Ready in:

Ingredients

- 1/2 cup chopped fresh strawberries
- 1 tablespoon confectioner's sugar
- 7 large basil leaves
- 1 1/2 ounces New Amsterdam gin
- white grape Champagne (I used Mumm Napa Blanc de Blancs)

Direction

- Chop the strawberries into small pieces and place in a small container or bowl.
- Add the sugar to the chopped strawberries and mix well. Let the mixture sit on the countertop for about 10-15 minutes to allow

the sugar to draw the juices out of the strawberries.

- Place the basil leaves in a cocktail shaker and pour the strawberry sugar mixture over them.
- Using a wooden muddler, gently begin muddling the mixture, pressing firmly so the basil leaves release their oils while also creating a strawberry purée.
- When the purée is sufficiently muddled, fill the shaker 2/3 full with ice.
- Add the gin and shake vigorously until mixed.
- Strain the mixture into a martini glass. (The purée will be thick, so it will take longer to get the liquid out, but your patience will pay off.)
- Pour Champagne into the mixture to fill the glass. Enjoy responsibly!

102. Strawberry Champagne Mousse

Serving: Serves 8 | Prep: | Cook: | Ready in:

Ingredients

- 4 full cups fresh quatered strawberries
- 1/3 cup of sugar
- 2 packets of plain gelatin
- 1/4 cup of champagne
- 4 tablespoons of flattened champagne

Direction

- Mash strawberries with a masher
- Add sugar and gently mix
- Dissolve gelatin in flattened champagne over low heat, avoid boiling
- Add dissolved warm gelatin to mashed strawberries
- Whip the mixture with hand mixer on medium to high speed for 4 minutes
- Add 1/4 cup or a splash of champagne into whipped mixture, and gently mix it in
- Spoon into ramekins
- Let the mousse settle at room temperature for 30 to 40 minutes

103. Strawberry Juice And A Champagne Cocktail

Serving: Makes about 2 cups strawberry puree, enough for 8 to 10 drinks | Prep: | Cook: |Ready in:

Ingredients

- 1 quart ripe strawberries, rinsed and hulled
- 1/4 cup superfine sugar (plus more, depending on the sweetness of your berries)
- Squeeze of lemon juice
- Champagne (optional -- and not a really expensive bottle, but no swill!)

Direction

- Put the strawberries, sugar and lemon juice in a blender and puree until smooth. Taste for sweetness, and add more sugar if you like.
- Once it tastes right, you can pass the puree through a fine sieve to get rid of the strawberry seeds if you like (I don't, because I enjoy their crunch).
- If you're making strawberry juice, stir 3 tablespoons of the puree into about 5 ounces of cold water. Add ice if you like.
- To make a Rossini, put 3 tablespoons of the strawberry puree in a tumbler or a large wine glass. Pour a little Champagne into the glass, and combine with the puree by stirring gently with a spoon. Fill the glass with Champagne (it will foam up as you pour -- this is part of the fun) and serve immediately, preferably with some salty little cheese biscuits.

104. Strawberry And Ricotta Salad

Serving: Serves 4 | Prep: | Cook: |Ready in:

Ingredients

- For the Champagne vanilla dressing:
- 1 vanilla bean or 1 teaspoon vanilla extract
- 3/4 cup extra virgin olive oil
- 4 tablespoons Champagne vinegar
- 1 tablespoon hot water
- 1/2 tablespoon honey
- 1/2 teaspoon Dijon mustard
- For the salad:
- 2 cups sliced strawberries
- 2 cups baby arugula
- 2 ounces sheep's milk farmer's cheese (or ricotta cheese), crumbled
- 1 cup pistachios, shelled

Direction

- For the Champagne vanilla dressing:
- Split the vanilla bean and scrape out the seeds.
- Combine vanilla bean seeds, Champagne vinegar, honey, and Dijon mustard in a mixing bowl. Slowly add the extra virgin olive oil and hot water to mix, using a handheld blender on high.
- For the salad:
- Combine strawberries, arugula, and pistachios in a bowl. Add dressing to taste and toss salad.
- Transfer to individual salad plates, top with crumbled cheese, and serve.

105. Summer Salad With Grilled Shrimp

Serving: Serves 1 large salad | Prep: | Cook: |Ready in:

Ingredients

- The Shrimp
- 3-4 pieces of garlic, minced or put through a garlic press
- 1 yellow onion, minced
- 1.5 teaspoons dry mustard
- 1.5 teaspoons dijon mustard
- 2 lemons

- 1 bunch parsley, roughly chopped
- 1 handful chives, roughly chopped
- 1 handful basil, chiffonaded
- cayenne pepper
- kosher salt
- freshly ground black pepper
- 2 pounds raw shrimp (sized 12-16 or 16-20), peeled, de-tailed, and de-veined
- olive oil
- The Salad
- 4 ears corn, kernels shaved off
- 1 pint cherry tomatoes, halved
- 1/2 small red onion, finely diced
- 2-3 avocados, diced
- 1 head boston (bibb) lettuce, torn
- 5-6 leaves basil, chiffonaded
- 1 handful parsley, roughly chopped
- 1 bunch chives, chopped or snipped to 1/4" rounds
- 1 shallot, minced very finely
- extra virgin olive oil
- champagne vinegar
- kosher salt
- freshly ground black pepper

Direction

- The Shrimp
- Mix together garlic, onion, mustards, the juice of both lemons, all the herbs, and a few shakes of cayenne pepper. Add salt and pepper (enough so that you can see the pepper after you've mixed everything together). Add the shrimp, and olive oil enough to coat it all, and combine well. Cover and refrigerate forever. Ok a few hours will be just fine.
- Skewer the shrimp onto bamboo sticks (most grocery stores have 'em, and I like doing 4-6 shrimp/skewer), allowing whatever marinade sticks to stay on. Grill over a medium high heat for 2-4 minutes per side, or until they're pink and done and delicious, but not overcooked.
- The Salad
- In a large salad bowl, toss together corn, tomatoes, onion, avocados, and torn lettuce.

- Mix the herbs in a small bowl, season aggressively with salt and pepper, and add the shallot and a few tablespoons champagne vinegar. Let this sit for a moment, and then drizzle in olive oil until you have a delicious vinaigrette.
- Toss the vinaigrette with the salad, and add the grilled shrimp. Enjoy!

106. Summer Vegetable Flatbread

Serving: Serves 2 | Prep: | Cook: | Ready in:

Ingredients

- 2 pieces naan bread
- 10-12 stalks of asparagus
- 1 ear corn on the cob
- 6 ounces plain greek yogurt (one single serving cup)
- 1/2 teaspoon champagne vinegar
- 1/2 teaspoon honey
- Salt & Pepper
- Red pepper flakes, to your desired spice level

Direction

- Preheat the oven to 425° F. Bring a large pot of salted water to a boil.
- Place asparagus on a baking sheet (I like to line my sheet with foil). Drizzle olive oil on top and season with salt and pepper. Roast asparagus for 10-15 minutes. You want them to be cooked, but not too floppy. Keep a bit of bite in them. Cut into 2-inch pieces.
- While the asparagus is roasting, prepare the corn by removing the husks and any strings. Place the corn in the boiling salted water. When the water comes back to a boil, turn off the heat and cover the pot with a lid. After 3 minutes, remove corn from pot. When corn is cool enough to handle, hold the corn upright and use a knife to remove the kernels.

- Place naan in oven (or cook according to package directions). I kept mine in the oven for 3-5 minutes, until the bubbles started to brown and the naan was warm.
- Stir champagne vinegar and honey into yogurt until combined. Spoon onto naan evenly. Sprinkle with salt and pepper. Place corn and asparagus on top, and add red pepper flakes. Depending on how large your naan is, you can cut it into pieces or serve as is.

107.   Superstorm Vanilla Bourbon Champagne Cocktail

Serving: Makes 1 | Prep: | Cook: | Ready in:

Ingredients

- Janet Johnston' s Vanilla Sugar Cubes
- 4 vanilla beans
- 3 cups white sugar
- 1/4 cup pure vanilla extract
- Vanilla Bourbon Champagne Cocktail
- 1 vanilla bean cube
- 1 shot good bourbon whiskey (such as Maker's Mark)
- Chilled champagne or prosecco
- Split vanilla bean, for garnish

Direction

- Janet Johnston's Vanilla Sugar Cubes
- Cut the vanilla beans into 1/2-inch pieces and ground in a sprice mill until powdered.
- Mix together all ingredients. Scrape into a parchment-lined 8-inch pan to about a 1/2-inch depth. Use a knife to score into 1/2-inch cubes. Bake for 90 minutes at 275°F. Remove and let cool. Remove sugar and break into cubes.
- Alternatively, take an already-made sugar cube and put a couple wee drops of pure vanilla extract on it.
- Vanilla Bourbon Champagne Cocktail

- Drop a vanilla sugar cube into a chilled champagne flute. Add a shot of bourbon and fill the glass with champagne or Prosecco. Garnish with a split vanilla bean. Cheers!

108.   Tagliatelle With Shrimp And Champagne Butter Sauce

Serving: Serves 4 | Prep: | Cook: | Ready in:

Ingredients

- Champagne Butter Sauce
- 1/4 cup minced shallots
- 2 cups Champagne or other sparkling wine
- 2/3 cup cold butter, cut into 2-inch cubes
- Salt and pepper
- Tagliatelle and Shrimp
- 1 pound fresh tagliatelle, linguine, or spaghetti
- 1 tablespoon butter
- 1 large shallot, chopped
- 2 cloves garlic, chopped
- 1 pound shrimp
- Salt and pepper
- 1/4 cup Champagne or other sparkling white wine
- Chopped parsley, for garnish

Direction

- Make the Champagne butter sauce: combine the shallots and Champagne in a pan over medium-high heat. Boil, stirring occasionally, until reduced to a glaze. Whisk in cold butter cubes a few at a time until sauce is thickened slightly. (For a cleaner sauce you may want to strain the shallots out, but I like the sweet astringency they lend to the dish.)
- Cook the pasta in boiling water until al dente. Drain and return to the pot. Pour the Champagne butter sauce over the pasta and toss to combine. Set aside.
- Cook the shrimp: heat the butter in the same pan you made the Champagne butter sauce in

(this adds flavor and cuts down on dishes!). Add the shallots and garlic and cook until just softened. Add the shrimp and cook, stirring occasionally, until the shrimp turn pink and are cooked through (this will only take a few minutes). Season with salt and pepper and deglaze the pan with the Champagne. Stir once and transfer the entire contents to the pasta pot. Toss to combine.

- Serve the tagliatelle with shrimp and Champagne butter sauce in large shallow bowls. Garnish with parsley and serve immediately.

109.   Teatime With The Romanoffs

Serving: Serves 1 | Prep: | Cook: | Ready in:

Ingredients

- For the cocktail:
- 3/4 ounce vodka
- 1/2 ounce ginger syrup (recipe below)
- 1/2 ounce lime juice
- dry Champagne (or other sparkling wine)
- For the ginger syrup:
- 1/2 cup thinly sliced fresh ginger
- 1/2 cup demerera sugar (regular sugar is fine, too)
- 1/2 cup water

Direction

- For the cocktail:
- Shake all the ingredients except the Champagne with ice until chilled. Strain into a coupe or Champagne flute and top with the sparkling wine.
- For the ginger syrup:
- Combine all ingredients in a saucepan and bring to a boil, stirring to dissolve the sugar. Remove from the heat and allow to steep for at least an hour, then strain.

110.   Thai High

Serving: Makes one | Prep: | Cook: | Ready in:

Ingredients

- 2 ounces Vodka
- 3 ounces Orange Mango ICE water
- 1 piece Frozen Rasberry Champagne

Direction

- Pour Vodka in a martini glass
- Pour ICE water
- Float Raspberry Champagne cube on top

111.   The Bitter Frenchman

Serving: Serves 1 | Prep: | Cook: | Ready in:

Ingredients

- 1 ounce London dry-style gin
- 1/2 ounce Campari
- 1/2 ounce simple syrup
- 1/4 ounce lemon juice
- dry Champagne (or other dry sparkling wine)

Direction

- Shake all the ingredients except the Champagne with ice until chilled. Strain into a coupe or Champagne flute and top with the Champagne. Garnish with a lemon twist.

112.   The Final Countdown

Serving: Serves 1 | Prep: | Cook: | Ready in:

Ingredients

- 1/2 ounce London dry-style gin

- 1/2 ounce Green Chartreuse
- 1/2 ounce Luxardo Maraschino liqueur
- 1/2 ounce lime juice
- dry Champagne (or other dry sparkling wine)

Direction

- Shake all the ingredients except the Champagne with ice until chilled. Strain into a coupe or Champagne flute and top with the Champagne.

---

113.   The Monty Python

Serving: Makes 1 | Prep: | Cook: | Ready in:

Ingredients

- 1 ounce St. Germain (an elderflower-flavored liqueur)
- .5 ounces elderflower syrup (or simple syrup)
- Champagne/Prosecco

Direction

- Pour the St. Germain and elderflower syrup/simple syrup into champagne glass and fill with bubbles. Garnish and Enjoy!

---

114.   The Pear Fect Champagne Cocktail

Serving: Makes 1 drink | Prep: | Cook: | Ready in:

Ingredients

- 1 ounce pear nectar
- Splash cranberry juice
- champagne
- Sprig fresh rosemary for garnish
- fresh cranberries for garnish

Direction

- Fill a bowl with fresh cranberries and cover them with warm water. Let them sit for 10 minutes and then drain and pat them dry.
- Add 1 ounce pear nectar and a splash of cranberry juice to a champagne flute. Fill the rest of the flute with champagne and garnish with fresh cranberries and sprig of rosemary.

---

115.   The Resolution

Serving: Serves 1 | Prep: | Cook: | Ready in:

Ingredients

- Absinthe, for rinsing
- 2 dashes Peychaud's bitters
- 1 teaspoon orange liqueur, such as Pierre Ferrand Dry Orange Curacao, Grand Marnier, or Cointreau
- Champagne, or another dry sparkling wine
- 1 lemon twist

Direction

- Pour a very small amount of absinthe into a coupe glass. Swirl the glass to coat it with absinthe; then pour it out. (If you're making multiple Resolutions at once, you can pour the absinthe from this first glass into a second glass, swirl, then pour it into a third glass, etc.)
- To the rinsed glass, add the bitters and orange liqueur. Top up with Champagne. Garnish with a lemon twist, and serve immediately.

---

116.   The Ultimate Bite

Serving: Makes varies. most people will eat 2-3 as a passed appetizer | Prep: | Cook: | Ready in:

Ingredients

- container Dried Medjool dates sliced longways half through and pitted

- large wedge Stuff dates with generous amount of Clawson Dairy Blue Stilton
- 1 Glass of very cold champagne

Direction

- Partially slice the dried dates longways and remove the pit
- Insert generous amount of Stilton
- Serve with very cold glass of champagne or Blanc de Noirs

---

117.   Twice Cooked Sardines And Green Grape Gremolata

Serving: Serves 6 | Prep: | Cook: |Ready in:

Ingredients

- 6 fresh sardines
- 1/4 cup chopped parsley
- 2 tablespoons champagne vinegar
- 6 large cloves of garlic
- 1 lemon
- 3 tablespoons olive oil
- 1 tablespoon sesame oil
- 5 seconds of grating fresh nutmeg
- Dash black pepper
- 1 handful of green grapes, chopped

Direction

- Heat oven to 350 degrees.
- In a bowl, combine parsley, olive oil, juice from half of the lemon, chopped garlic, and champagne vinegar.
- Coarsely chop the ingredients in a food processor or with an immersion blender.
- To prepare the sardines, make sure they have been scaled and cleaned (i.e. removal of guts and back bone if possible) and give the little guys a good rinse before cooking. Leave head and tail on.
- Grate nutmeg for five seconds over both sides of the fish and pepper lightly.

- Heat sesame oil in non-stick pan over medium flame. Wait 2-3 minutes for the oil to get hot. To test if it is ready, flick some water into the pan and the oil should hiss.
- Add the sardines to the pan (it should be large enough for each sardine to touch the bottom). Sauté for 5 minutes. Flip the fish (it should be golden brown and crispy) and sauté the other side for five minutes as well.
- Line an oven-safe pan with thin slices of lemon and lay your crispy skin sardines on top.
- Cover the sardines with a coating of the parsley, lemon, vinegar, garlic mixture (the gremolata) and put in the oven for 5 minutes.
- Before removing from oven, turn broiler on low and move the fish to the top rack, directly below flame. Cook for 2 more minutes, allowing the skin to get the perfect crunch.
- To serve, plate fish over the remaining gremolata and cover with the chopped grapes. Dig in.

---

118.   Valentine's Strawberry Champagne

Serving: Makes 6 | Prep: | Cook: |Ready in:

Ingredients

- 1 bottle champagne
- 1 cup strawberries, fresh or frozen
- 1 lime

Direction

- If you're using frozen strawberries, defrost them. Wash and dry fresh strawberries. Puree strawberries with a stick blender until smooth. Squeeze juice of the lime and add to the puree.
- Place strawberry puree in tall glasses, about an inch high.
- Pour champagne over strawberry puree, then give the drinks a stir. Decorate with fresh strawberries and serve.

119. Wine Jelly, White Chocolate And Caviar Verrine

Serving: Serves 6-8 | Prep: | Cook: | Ready in:

Ingredients

- Wine Jelly, White Chocolate and Caviar Verrine
- 750ml Champagne or sparkling wine (I used Moscato)
- 100ml creme de cassis or other berry liqueur (I used cassis/blackcurrant cordial)
- 150g caster sugar
- 6 gelatine leaves
- White chocolate shavings (recipe below)
- Black caviar (I didn't use beluga.....)
- White Chocolate Shavings
- 100-200g White chocolate

Direction

- Wine Jelly, White Chocolate and Caviar Verrines
- Place six wine glasses or 8 small glasses in the deep freezer for 15 minutes.
- Soak the gelatine leaves in a small bowl of cold water for 3 minutes. {Alternatively, follow the instructions on your pack of gelatine leaves. You can also use gelatine powder, adjust the required amount according to the volume of liquid you're using}.
- Open the champagne/wine, pour 150 ml into a pan, and reseal the bottle with a wine cork. {This is where things could have gone really wrong for me as my cork broke. Thankfully, I had some Ikea wine corks to hand when I finally extracted the fragments of a once-whole cork!}
- Add the sugar and creme de cassis/cassis cordial to the champagne/wine and gently heat, stirring until the sugar has dissolved (without letting it boil or even get too hot). Remove from the heat.
- Squeeze the excess water from the gelatine leaves and add to the mixture, whisking continuously until dissolved. Pour into a jug. Pour around 50 ml into each glass, and slowly and gently top with champagne/wine, trying to minimize the frothing. Return the glasses to the freezer for 20 minutes, then transfer to the fridge and leave overnight before serving.
- {I used two shapes of glasses. One formed nice bubbles as soon as they came out of the freezer (Ellipse-shaped glasses). The others didn't (Tumblers). Because I'd read the trails and travails of those who had gone before me, I knew that there was still time for things to go 'right'.}
- And 'right' they did! I kept nudging them a bit 'til I went to bed, just giving the glasses a little shake and truly, the next morning, they all had bubbles in them. It was interesting to note though that the jelly in the Ellipse glasses formed differently (individual bubbles) from those in the tumblers (bubble chains).
- White Chocolate Shavings
- When Heston pairs his white chocolate with beluga, he suggests making round discs of chocolate. To quote: '... the sensation of these sweets is heightened if you place the chocolate and caviar disc on the tongue, close your mouth and leave to melt. As the chocolate melts, the caviar flavour comes through gradually. You will be amazed by the pleasure of the changing flavours and sensations'. I preferred to make shavings of mine because I wanted melt-in-your-mouth to go with the jelly.
- Melt chocolate in a bain marie {safer than scorching and ruining it in the microwave!}
- Once melted, spread on a silicone mat (or a cold, stone surface.)
- Refrigerate it at this point...if it's on a mat.
- When cold, use a sharp knife to draw out/shave into curls. You can also cut out disks and other shapes.

120.   Winter Salad

Serving: Serves 4-6 | Prep: | Cook: |Ready in:

Ingredients

- The Salad
- 2 bunches of watercress
- 1 piece blue castello or other mild creamy blue cheese
- 1/2 cup candied walnuts
- 2 pink grapefruits
- 1 tablespoon currants
- 1 shallot, thinly sliced
- 2 tablespoons champagne vinegar
- 1 teaspoon red vinegar
- 6 tablespoons olive oil
- sea salt and freshly ground black pepper
- Candied Walnuts
- 1 cup walnut pieces (mostly halves)
- 2 tablespoons maple syrup
- 1 tablespoon sugar
- 1/2 teaspoon kosher sea salt
- 1/4 teaspoon freshly ground black pepper
- 1 pinch cayenne

Direction

- The Salad
- Combine 1 tbsp hot water and red vinegar in a very small bowl with 1 tbsp currants.
- In another very small bowl, toss champagne vinegar with the sliced shallot.
- Wash and dry the leaves of watercress and mound on a large platter.
- Cut the Blue Castello into small pieces, removing any rind, and strew over leaves.
- With a very sharp knife cut the top and bottom off the grapefruit. Cut off all the rind and pith. Over a medium sized bowl, carefully slice between the membranes to remove the fruit in sections, catching any juice and the fruit in the bowl.
- Arrange the sectioned grapefruit over the salad.
- Toss the walnuts over the top.

- Lift the shallots out of the vinegar carefully, reserving the vinegar for the dressing. Pulling the rings apart, scatter the shallots over the salad.
- Drain the currants, and toss over the salad.
- Add 1-2 tbsp grapefruit juice to the small bowl with the champagne vinegar. Whisk in olive oil, 1/2 tsp sea salt, and a few grindings black pepper. Dress the salad - you may not need all the dressing.
- Candied Walnuts
- Preheat the oven to 325.
- Toss all ingredients together in a medium sized bowl.
- Lightly spray a rimmed cookie sheet with vegetable oil.
- Spread the coated nuts over the cookie sheet.
- Toast for 15 minutes, stirring every 5 minutes.
- Remove from oven and cool stirring every few minutes so they don't stick too badly to the pan.

121.   Zuni Café Bread Salad With Currants, Pine Nuts, Scallions & Roasted Chicken

Serving: Serves 4 | Prep: 0hours20mins | Cook: 1hours0mins |Ready in:

Ingredients

- 8 ounces slightly stale open-crumbed, chewy, peasant-style bread (not sourdough)
- 6 tablespoons to 8 tablespoons mild-tasting olive oil
- 1 1/2 tablespoons Champagne vinegar or white wine vinegar
- 1 pinch salt and freshly cracked black pepper
- 2 teaspoons pine nuts
- 2 to 3 garlic cloves, slivered
- 1/4 cup slivered scallions (about 4 scallions), including a little of the green part

- 1 tablespoon dried currants plumped in 1 tablespoon red wine vinegar and 1 tablespoon warm water for 10 minutes or so
- 2 tablespoons lightly salted chicken stock or lightly salted water
- 1 roasted chicken (we like Barbara Kafka's: https://food52.com/recipes...)
- 3 handfuls A few handfuls of arugula, frisée, or red mustard greens, carefully washed and dried

Direction

- Preheat the broiler. Carve off all of the bottom and most of the top and side crusts from your bread (you can reserve these to use as croutons for soup or another salad). Tear bread into irregular 2- to 3-inch chunks—you should get about 4 cups.
- Toss them with a tablespoon or two of olive oil, lightly coating them, and broil very briefly, just to lightly color the edges. If you'd like to toast the pine nuts (recommended) you can put them on your broiler tray as well, but watch them very carefully because they cook quickly!
- Combine about 1/4 cup of the olive oil with the Champagne or white wine vinegar and salt and pepper to taste. Toss about 1/4 cup of this tart vinaigrette with the torn toasted bread in a wide salad bowl; the bread will be unevenly dressed. Taste one of the more saturated pieces. If it is bland, add a little salt and pepper and toss again.
- Heat a spoonful of the olive oil in a small skillet, add the garlic and scallions, and cook over medium-low heat, stirring constantly, until softened. Don't let them color. Scrape into the bread and fold to combine. Drain the plumped currants and fold them in, along with the pine nuts, if they were not already mixed with the bread scraps from the broiling step. Dribble the chicken stock or lightly salted water over the salad and fold again.
- Taste a few pieces of bread—a fairly saturated one and a dryish one. If it is bland, add salt, pepper, and/or a few drops of vinegar, then

toss well. When the chicken comes out of the oven, drizzle the bread with a spoonful or two more of chicken pan juices and toss. Add the greens, a drizzle of vinaigrette, and fold well. Taste again.
- Pile the bread salad on the serving dish. Carve the roast chicken and plunk the pieces on top of the salad, using more pan juices to moisten the bread as needed.

122. Pecan Crusted Goat Cheese Salad With Blood Orange Tahini Dressing

Serving: Makes 4 main course servings | Prep: | Cook: | Ready in:

Ingredients

- For the Dressing
- 1/2 cup sunflower seed oil
- 1/4 cup champagne vinegar
- Juice from one blood orange
- Juice from one tangerine
- 2 tablespoons dried cherries
- 1 tablespoon tahini
- 1 tablespoon honey
- 1 teaspoon sea salt
- For the Salad
- 1.5 cups forbidden rice, uncooked
- 2 pounds boneless, skinless chicken breasts
- 1 tablespoon Datil Pepper Spice OR 1 teaspoon each sea salt and pepper
- 1 tablespoon olive oil
- 1.5 cups chicken stock
- 3 blood oranges, divided (one for the braise; two for the salad)
- 5 ounces goat cheese
- 1 cup pecans, divided (1/2 cup for the salad, 1/2 cup crushed for the goat cheese)
- 8 cups baby arugula, cleaned and dried
- 1 cup fresh basil leaves, whole
- 1 cup dried tart cherries

Direction

- For the Dressing
- Put the sunflower seed oil, champagne vinegar, juice from both a blood orange and tangerine, dried cherries, tahini, honey and salt in your blender and blend on high speed until the cherries are broken up and the mixture is completely emulsified. Set aside.
- For the Salad
- Preheat the oven to 400 degrees F. Make sure you have a rack in the middle of the oven.
- Cut one blood orange in half. One half will be used to squeeze over the chicken prior to the oven; the other half needs to be thinly sliced.
- Grab two large plates: one for your raw chicken (in which to season it on) and another to rest the chicken after you've browned it.
- Place the chicken on one of the plates and coat with 1 tablespoon Datil spice or 1 teaspoon each sea salt and pepper.
- Heat either a large cast-iron pot (I use a 5.5 QT cocotte) or Dutch oven over medium-high heat. Add 1 tablespoons of olive oil. Once it's shimmering, swirl it around so that it coats the surface.
- Place the chicken in the pot, without crowding it. You may need to brown the chicken in batches depending on the size of your pot. Leave the chicken, undisturbed, for 2-3 minutes or until a nice brown crust forms. Flip and repeat on the other side. Remove from the pan and place on the other clean plate. Repeat until all breasts are browned, but not cooked through.
- Pour the chicken broth into the pot, scraping the bottom with a wooden spoon to get up any brown bits.
- Add the chicken and accumulated juices to the pot. Squeeze half of one blood orange over the chicken and then place the blood orange slices from the other half in and round the chicken.
- Place the pot on the middle rack of the oven, with the lid on, and cook for 25 minutes or until the chicken is cooked through.
- Set the chicken aside to cool.

- Once cooled, cut the chicken into small, bite-size chunks.
- Cook your rise according to the instructions on the package. Set aside to cool.
- Grab your crushed pecans, goat cheese and a plate to rest the balls on. Make sure your pecans are finely crushed up. Roll about 1 teaspoon of goat cheese into a ball between your palms. Gently roll the goat cheese balls in the crushed pecans and place on the plate. Once all of the goat cheese is coated and rolled, place the plate in the freezer. After 1-2 hours, they should be frozen and you can place them in a resealable plastic bag and put back in the freezer. Take them out of the freezer 2 hours prior to serving the salad.
- Peel and thinly slice crosswise the remaining two blood oranges.
- Put the arugula in a large bowl. Sprinkle the rice, basil leaves, pecans, cherries and chicken. Drizzle with half of the salad dressing and toss a bit. Taste. Do you need all of the dressing? Everyone's taste is different. Add more in small increments until you hit the sweet spot. Place the blood orange slices around the salad and sprinkle with the pecan-crusted goat cheese balls. That's it. You're done.
- This should be eaten within an hour of tossing...arugula + dressing won't last long together once introduced. That's just how some relationships go. Enjoy!

---

123.   "Southern Belle Ini"

Serving: Serves 1 | Prep: | Cook: |Ready in:

Ingredients

- 4 ounces Champagne
- 2 splashes Ocean Spray White Peach Cranberry Juice
- 2 pieces frozen raspberries
- 1 pinch red sugar crystals

Direction

- 1. Lightly dampen the rims of the champagne glasses with a little bit of water.
- 2. Pour color sugar crystals onto a plate and roll the rim of the glasses in the sugar coating the rims.
- 3. Fill the champagne glasses a little over halfway full.
- 4. Add a few splashes of the juice to top them off (more or less depending on preference.)
- 5. Finished off the drink by adding a few frozen raspberries.

Index

Zest 13,39

Conclusion

Thank you again for downloading this book!

I hope you enjoyed reading about my book!

If you enjoyed this book, please take the time to share your thoughts and post a review on Amazon. It'd be greatly appreciated!

Write me an honest review about the book – I truly value your opinion and thoughts and I will incorporate them into my next book, which is already underway.

Thank you!

If you have any questions, **feel free to contact at:** _author@sauterecipes.com_

Wendy Beran

sauterecipes.com

Printed in Great Britain
by Amazon

82878125R00045